ACCLAIM
SMART QUESTIONS TO ASK YOUR LAWYER

"This invaluable book contains more than just 'smart questions'. It gives readers basic, commonsense advice to guide them in every major role they play: as parents and spouses, as buyers and sellers, as businessmen and women, and as just plain citizens. In the end, both client and lawyer are well served."

—George Gross, Executive Vice President for Government Affairs, Magazine Publishers of America

"A source of comfort to people trembling on the brink of consulting lawyers . . . I heartily recommend it."

—Raoul Lionel Felder, from the law firm of Raoul Lionel Felder, P.C., New York City

"A good starting point for anyone who feels they may need a lawyer and a reminder to attorneys that clients need information, too! Communication is a two-way street and this easy-to-read book certainly demonstrates that point."

—Jeanne Schubert Barnum, President, National Association of Women Lawyers

The SMART QUESTIONS series

Published by HarperPaperbacks

ATTENTION: ORGANIZATIONS AND CORPORATIONS

Most HarperPaperbacks are available at special quantity discounts for bulk purchases for sales promotions, premiums, or fund-raising. For information, please call or write:
Special Markets Department, HarperCollins Publishers,
10 East 53rd Street, New York, N.Y. 10022.
Telephone: (212) 207-7528. Fax: (212) 207-7222.

SMART QUESTIONS TO ASK YOUR LAWYER

DOROTHY LEEDS
WITH SUE BELEVICH SCHILLING

HarperPaperbacks
A Division of HarperCollins*Publishers*

If you purchased this book without a cover, you should be aware that this book is stolen property. It was reported as "unsold and destroyed" to the publisher and neither the author nor the publisher has received any payment for this "stripped book."

HarperPaperbacks   *A Division of* HarperCollins*Publishers*
10 East 53rd Street, New York, N.Y. 10022

Copyright © 1992 by Dorothy Leeds
All rights reserved. No part of this book may be used or reproduced in any manner whatsoever without written permission of the publisher, except in the case of brief quotations embodied in critical articles and reviews. For information address HarperCollins*Publishers,*
10 East 53rd Street, New York, N.Y. 10022.

Cover illustration by Richard Rossiter

First printing: April 1992

Printed in the United States of America

HarperPaperbacks and colophon are trademarks of HarperCollins*Publishers*

❖ 10 9 8 7 6 5 4

To Jack Strauss, lawyer extraordinaire, who is always there, brilliantly and patiently, for his family, friends, and lucky clients. Thank you Jack, for everything.

ACKNOWLEDGMENTS

Special thank-yous to:
Karen Solem, a great lady and a great editor.
Chris Wilhide, who was always there when we needed her.
Barbara Lowenstein, who made this series possible.
Norman Kurz, for his excellence, kindness, and patience.

Sue Schilling and I both want to express our appreciation
for Sharyn Kolberg, whose calm demeanor and excellent
writing skills make it all seem easy.

CONTENTS

INTRODUCTION

When you're in need of legal advice, how do you choose the lawyer best qualified to help you out of your current difficulties? If a lawyer is drawing up a legal document for you, do you always understand everything that's in it? How do you know the strategy your lawyer is recommending to win your lawsuit is the right one for you? You don't know . . . unless you *ask questions*!

Often the need to ask questions is strongest when you are most vulnerable. You probably don't have lawyers on retainer—you might seek one out when you're in trouble, or have a problem you can't solve. You may be angry and feel victimized when you look for legal counsel; you want someone to tell you how the wrong can be righted. You might feel that you have been taken advantage of and seek legal redress.

When you're angry and upset, you may not be thinking clearly. When you're in trouble or feel victimized, you're likely to feel frightened; you don't ask as many questions as you should. Consequently, you don't get the information you need.

Yet this is just the time you need all the information you can get. You're probably being asked to make difficult decisions—decisions that may affect the rest of your life, and the lives of your family members as well.

Take divorce, for instance. Even the "friendliest" of divorces creates emotional anxiety for everyone involved. And if there are children to be considered, it is your right, as well as your responsibility, to obtain the best possible information for everyone's present and future well-being.

There's no need to let others have control over your legal affairs, to allow anyone else to make decisions for you, or to feel that you are a victim of circumstance. This book was written to help you go from victim to victor, and to show you how you can become a "questioning detective," uncovering the clues you need to make the best decisions.

LEARN TO PROTECT YOURSELF

People learn many things in law school. They learn about the law, of course, but they also learn how to think in a particular way. They learn to become tough, and how to look out for themselves as well as their clients.

I don't mean to say that every lawyer is only out for him or herself, or that lawyers don't care about their clients. I do mean that in order for you to get the most out of your relationship with your lawyer, and to get the best legal representation, you must learn to be tough yourself, and to think the way lawyers think. In order to do that, you need to be an "informed consumer" about the law and about your rights under the law.

The problem is that the law is so complicated, and you're constantly being bombarded with new information. And when you find yourself in a face-to-face situation where you need specific—and vitally important—information, all the facts, figures, advice, and opinions you've heard before fly right out the window. What can you do? How can you find out, right then and there, what you need to know?

You can ask questions.

There are only two ways to get information. One is by watching and reading. The other is by asking questions. You might get some clues about a lawyer by observing his or her behavior in the office. You can probably read up on the law and how it pertains to your situation. This is fine for preparation and background information, but the only way to get immediate information, direct from the source's mouth and directly applicable to your own problem, is by asking questions.

WHY DON'T WE ASK MORE?

The reason we don't ask more questions is largely because we're afraid to question authority. We follow the tradition that says "the lawyer knows best." We're afraid to doubt his or her advice.

We're reluctant to ask questions because:

- we think the law is so complicated we couldn't understand it anyway;
- we assume all lawyers are competent just because they have a law degree;
- many lawyers are expensive and we don't want to pay for the "extra time" questions may take up.

Lawyers know the power of questions. Our whole legal system is based on gaining information through a process of questions and answers. There have been hundreds of television shows and movies portraying lawyers as quick-thinking questioning experts. This book will provide you with the tools to become a questioning expert and get the information you need.

BUT WHAT DO I ASK?

Many times we don't ask questions because we're not sure what we should be asking. We figure, these people are the experts, they know what they're talking about. "I'm paying my lawyer to handle this for me. She's the one who knows the law—and besides, I don't even know what questions to ask."

We are faced with difficult decisions every time we seek out legal advice, and often we come away with lingering doubts. "Was there something else I should have asked?" is the haunting refrain most of us have experienced after leaving the lawyer's office.

You might wish you had an expert with you to get the necessary information. Well, now you have. This book will turn *you* into the expert. Take it with you to the lawyer's office. Or write down the pertinent questions that apply to your situation. For example, if you're about to enter into a contract with someone, concentrate on the section called "The Small Print"; if you're contemplating divorce, turn to "Crimes of the Heart."

Some of the questions are for you to ask yourself (for instance, when choosing a lawyer, you may have to ask yourself if you prefer a more aggressive attorney or one with a gentler approach). Some questions are presented for your general knowledge about the law (such as the section on Ethics and Behavior). The bulk of the questions are for you to ask the lawyer.

In writing this book, we set out to explore some of the key issues that are on people's minds. We tried to cover as many areas of the law as we could. There's no way we could address every possible problem, but we tried to set up the questions using examples that most people could relate to.

Every question opens up other questions. Add your own questions to the list. We don't presume to have covered every possible legal situation. But the questions here should get you started, and should stimulate your own questioning process so that you, too, can get the information you really need.

WHY YOU NEED THIS BOOK

The purpose of this book is threefold:

1. To provide you with the questions to ask in order to get the information you need;
2. To get you into the habit of asking questions; and
3. To build your confidence in dealing with your lawyer.

After all, the person who asks the questions sets the direction and the topic in a discussion, and gains a sense of control in a difficult situation. Most psychologists agree that anxiety arises from loss of control. When you ask a question, the other person feels compelled to answer, and the power goes to the asker. (Just watch the power shift when someone asks you, "Where are you going?" and you answer, "Why do you ask?")

You don't have to take the lawyer's word for something just because he's a lawyer, or nod and say yes if you don't understand. You don't have to leave the office until you get a satisfactory answer, no matter how intimidating the lawyer may appear. You have the right to ask questions and the right to get answers. If a particular lawyer won't answer your questions, get one who will. If a lawyer says he doesn't have time for explanations, there are other lawyers around who are willing and able to do so.

A VERY WILLING LAWYER

I was very fortunate in writing this book to have found a lawyer who was not only willing and able to answer questions, but to ask them as well. Sue Belevich Schilling has been involved in the legal profession since 1974, when she was a paralegal working her way through law school. A graduate of St. John's University School of Law, Sue was admitted to the New York State Bar in 1980. She is currently in private practice in Syosset, New York, concentrating in the areas of real-estate law, wills and estate administration, business and corporate law, dispute resolutions, and general practice. She's also a volunteer firefighter, emergency medical technician, and an avid sports participant.

We share the same philosophy about the legal profession—that the lawyer and the client should establish a partnership. Lawyers are human, too, and may not always realize that they're intimidating, or that a client hasn't understood everything that's been said. Clear, comprehensive communication is part of a lawyer's business, and one of her most important functions.

I found communicating with Sue Schilling easy and fun. She's not at all the intimidating authority figure we often imagine lawyers to be. She's warm and compassionate and has a real desire to help anyone in trouble.

Sue and I don't claim to have exhausted all the questions you could, or should, ask about the law. Nor do we intend to give you specific legal advice. We have provided questions and examples to give you a basis for comparison: we didn't want to simply provide you with a list of questions and let it go at that. We wanted you to understand why each of the questions is important and what you should expect to learn from your lawyer's answer. When you ask a question, you may want to compare your lawyer's answer with the one in the book.

WHERE DO YOU LIVE?

This is one smart question you need to ask yourself as you're reading this book. Although we've tried to answer questions generically, the fact is that many laws vary from state to state. If you ask your lawyer a question from this book and her answer is different from the one we've provided, the difference may be due to variance in your state law. Once again, ask your lawyer to explain the law to you as it pertains to your home state.

THE HE/SHE ISSUE

One last word on a technical issue. We did not want to include any gender bias in this book by constantly using "he" to refer to the lawyer. On the other hand, it is very awkward to use "he/she" and "him or her" throughout. So when referring to "the lawyer," we use "he" in some examples and "she" in others.

This is your opportunity to create a new relationship with your lawyer, and with your prerogatives under the law. Be an active participant in the most important areas of your life. Lawyers are there to protect your rights—and you have the right to a clear and comprehensive understanding of everything that affects you. Make sure you stand up for that right, and start asking smart questions.

LEGAL REPRESENTATION: SMART QUESTIONS TO ASK WHEN CHOOSING A LAWYER

THE LAW IN OUR LIVES

Almost everything we do in life or death involves the law. Laws and legal principles are the rules that govern conduct between people, companies, the behavior society expects of us, and the obligations that government owes to us.

We might not spend most of our time thinking about it, but laws and legal principles come into play when we marry, divorce, have children, purchase consumer goods, homes, or other property, make investments, open businesses, hire and fire employees, deal with the government, enter into agreements, dispose of wastes, operate automobiles, are the victim of or are accused of crimes, receive medical treatment, refuse medical treatment, and make plans to dispose of our assets after death.

HOW DO YOU KNOW IF YOU NEED A LAWYER?

Life would not be much if the law became the predominant force in your life. Nevertheless, the law can protect you, direct you to behave in a certain way, or be used by others as a powerful weapon against you. Many people do not know or recognize when they should be paying attention to the law.

Here are some smart questions you should ask yourself to determine whether or not a situation warrants a lawyer's assistance:

Are you considering an important decision?

Very often your experience in your personal, business, or professional affairs makes you knowledgeable about legal issues even though you are not a lawyer. For example, if you're an employer, chances are you're aware of your basic obligations regarding withholding taxes, workers' compensation, employment benefits, discrimination, and discharge. If you own a business that involves disposable waste, you're probably familiar with government laws and regulations about protecting the environment. If you are a knowledgeable consumer, you know what to do if a product you buy doesn't work properly.

We are generally familiar with legal issues surrounding matters about which we have experience. However, important decisions that are not routine often have important legal consequences. It's when you're involved in important decisions outside your areas of expertise and experience that you need to consult a lawyer.

Is someone suing you?

You should consult an attorney when you are notified that someone may be or is starting a lawsuit against you.

Has someone damaged you or breached (broken; gone back on) a duty?

This can happen in personal, commercial, or professional circumstances. The instances where you may have a claim or lawsuit against someone else are almost limitless. Do you have problems with your marriage or the custody of your children? What if your insurance policy carrier won't honor its obligations? Do you have questions about a commercial contract or investments with friends or strangers? Are you involved in a dispute over real estate? Has the government refused to give you the benefits you deserve or tried to take your property or liberty? Was your doctor, dentist, accountant, or lawyer negligent? Has a product, be it a drug, appliance, or piece of equipment, injured you? In all of these cases, lawsuits may be involved and you should consult an attorney.

Are you involved in a criminal matter?

If you are the victim of a crime, you should either go directly to the appropriate law enforcement agency or consult your attorney, who will advise you which law enforcement agency you should contact. If you are arrested for a crime, you need a lawyer if it entails anything more than a small fine. If a jail term or a permanent bad mark on your record is involved, a lawyer is advised.

Do you need help accomplishing an important goal?

Has your marriage deteriorated and do you seek a divorce? Are you buying or selling real estate? Do you need relief from your creditors? Do you want to change your name? If you have specific goals you want accomplished, a lawyer will have the knowledge to help you accomplish them in a more expeditious fashion than if you tried to do these things yourself.

The only way you can find out if a lawyer is right for you is by asking questions. You may not choose to ask the lawyer all of the questions in this section. But you do want to ask enough questions to get the information you need. You also want to find out how willing this lawyer is to answer any questions you might have, and how you react to this lawyer's manner and attitudes.

Choosing a lawyer is a very important decision; if a lawyer does not understand your need to ask questions, then perhaps you should look somewhere else.

CHOOSING A LAWYER

Here's the setup: You've recently been transferred to a new job in a midsize city in a state you've never even visited before. Unfortunately, you and your husband have been having difficulties for quite a while, and you decide that a divorce is the only answer. Where do you go?

You look in the phone book. There are many names listed, none of which means anything to you. Should you start with Amos Allen, Esq., and go straight through to Zoë Zelig, Esq.?

You don't know very many people in this city, so you decide to ask some coworkers for recommendations. You get three different names. The dilemma still remains, how do you choose?

Here are some general questions that may help you before you begin your search:

CAN ANY LAWYER REPRESENT ME?

Just like doctors, some attorneys are general practitioners and some specialize or concentrate in one or only a few areas of the law. Few lawyers regularly practice in every area of the law.

While some firms are "full service" law firms, few lawyers are skilled in all areas. If you have a particular problem and know one or more lawyers you believe to be honest, intelligent, and professional, you should contact this lawyer, describe your problem, and ask for a referral. An experienced lawyer will be able to network and help you locate a lawyer who is qualified to work on your problem.

SHOULD I ASK FRIENDS AND RELATIVES?

Ask friends and relatives whose judgment you trust. Sometimes close friends and relatives have excellent judgment and life experiences that make them reliable advisers, especially if they have had problems similar to yours.

Getting recommendations is probably the best way to begin. It gives you a place to start, and you can use the recommended lawyer as a basis for comparison. But choosing a lawyer is a very personal decision, and you should not choose one based solely on another person's recommendation.

ARE THERE DIRECTORIES AND REFERRAL SERVICES?

There are nationally recognized legal directories that list highly rated law firms by city and state and describe the background and experience of all lawyers in all those firms. If a firm or lawyer to whom you are referred is not listed in one of these directories, that doesn't mean that he or she is not highly qualified, however. Not every good lawyer "advertises" by having his or her name listed with a referral service or legal directory (your lawyer may be so busy with local referrals that she doesn't have to seek additional work elsewhere).

CAN I CONSULT LOCAL BAR GROUPS?

Your local bar association may be able to refer you to a lawyer who specializes, or has had experience in the type of problem you're having. Bar associations can furnish you with basic information about an attorney, such as area of practice, geographic location, and when she was admitted to practice law. You will have to call the attorney yourself to ask additional questions and find out if the attorney is right for you and the problem you're having.

HOW CAN I SELECT A COMPASSIONATE LAWYER?

A lawyer is there to give you legal advice and to provide you with the best possible legal representation available. A lawyer is not trained to be a therapist or a marriage counselor. However, it may be comforting to you to choose an attorney who will treat you with respect and dignity and who will be sensitive to your troubled situation. A smart question to ask, however, is: just because you feel comfortable with a lawyer, does that mean he or she is the most effective lawyer for your case?

You may wish to (and probably should) interview several attorneys before making a choice. Ask your friends about their experiences with this attorney, or observe the attorney to see how she or he treats you at the initial interview.

Some considerations might be: Does the attorney cut you off in midsentence, or does she let you finish your thought before responding? Does the lawyer take other telephone calls while in a meeting with you, or does he devote complete attention to you? Does the lawyer have set answers for each problem you explain, or does he offer several options for you to choose? Does the attorney try to dominate the relationship, or does she let you have some input? Often a "gut" reaction about an attorney is correct; if he or she seems to be too busy to focus on your problems, maybe this is not the attorney for you.

WHAT CAN I DO IF I CAN'T AFFORD A LAWYER?

If you're accused of a crime and you cannot afford a lawyer, the court will appoint you one, free of charge. Your local criminal court system will maintain a public defender's office from whom you can get free representation.

If you have a civil (i.e., noncriminal) problem, you may also be able to get low-cost or no-cost legal representation if you meet certain low-income qualifications. Contact your local bar association; many have organized "pro bono" (free or low-cost civil legal services) programs, for which lawyers volunteer their time or agree to accept cases on a low-cost basis. Ultimately, you do have the right to represent yourself in your own legal affairs; however, lawyers are specially trained to assist you in handling your legal matters and will often save you time, aggravation, and money.

WHAT IS YOUR BACKGROUND OR EXPERIENCE?

You want to find out about the background of the lawyer and the experience of other professionals in the firm with respect to the area of law that pertains to your problem. You probably don't want a corporate tax attorney handling your divorce case if he's never done such a thing before; on the other hand, you want to know that a divorce attorney is well versed in any tax problems that may be related to divorce cases.

HAVE YOU HANDLED ANY CASES SIMILAR TO MINE BEFORE?

The attorney you are speaking with may be a graduate of an Ivy League law school and be wearing an expensive three-piece suit, but he may not have handled any cases like yours before. Suppose you want to have a conservator (someone who handles another person's affairs) appointed to handle your elderly mother's affairs. It could be that this attorney has handled estates on behalf of deceased persons, but never any conservatorship proceedings on behalf of persons still living. You should know this up front. This doesn't mean that the attorney will not be able to do a terrific job on your case—it means you need to ask more questions.

IF YOU DON'T HAVE EXPERIENCE IN HANDLING CASES LIKE MINE, WHAT STEPS WILL YOU TAKE TO HANDLE MY MATTER COMPETENTLY?

A lawyer who takes on your case will have an obligation either to become competent in the new area or to retain the services of a second attorney who is competent to solve your problem.

If your attorney says that she will become competent in handling your problem, ask whether you will be billed for this "educational" time, and, if so, will it be at a reduced rate. If your inexperienced attorney intends to consult another "expert" attorney, ask whether the services of the expert will be paid out of the fee quoted to you or whether you will have to pay extra for the "expert."

You should only have to pay one fair attorney's fee for your matter. You should not have to pay extra because your attorney must become educated in your area of the law or because there are two attorneys instead of one working on your case. Sometimes it may be necessary for more than one attorney to work on a complicated case that involves several areas of the law. Ask your attorney to explain why another attorney is being brought in to work on your case, and what additional fees you can expect to pay.

WHAT SPECIFIC LEGAL ISSUES NEED TO BE ADDRESSED AS A RESULT OF MY PROBLEM?

The lawyer's response to this question should tell you whether or not you have perceived the problem correctly prior to the consultation. For instance, you may have been fighting with your brothers and sisters over the handling of your deceased mother's estate. Although you may think you have a complicated legal problem, all you may need is a good mediator to settle your squabbles.

ARE THERE ANY OTHER ISSUES IN MY BUSINESS, PERSONAL, OR PROFESSIONAL LIFE THAT COULD BE AFFECTED BY THIS LEGAL PROBLEM?

Asking this question not only gives you information, it gives you an idea of how well versed this lawyer is with respect to your problem. Even if an attorney is not an expert in all the areas of law involved, he should point out all the issues to you and suggest a course of action.

For instance, as stated earlier, divorce not only deals with the issues of child custody, child support, and alimony, it deals with issues of property and tax as well. The attorney should point this out to you, and perhaps suggest that you consult with your accountant for answers to questions about taxes.

IF OTHER AREAS OF MY LIFE ARE AFFECTED, DO YOU HAVE EXPERIENCE IN THOSE AREAS?

The depth of the lawyer's experience in these other areas of law or the experience of his or her colleagues at the law firm may be a factor in your selection. If you are being sued, you'll need a lawyer who handles litigation matters (some attorneys do not). If you also own a business and need business advice from time to time, and this lawyer or a member of her firm is experienced in giving business advice, she could be a good choice for you. Even if this attorney does not have experience in the other areas, she may be able to refer you to someone who does—either in her law firm or elsewhere.

WHAT STRATEGY DO YOU RECOMMEND?

You can learn a lot from your lawyer by listening to his answers to your questions. The answers will tell you about his analytical ability, judgment, persuasiveness, and personality. Ask how the lawyer would approach the situation, and what the principal obstacles are to achieving a successful result. The answers will show you how he sizes up the strengths and weakness of your position.

ARE THERE OTHER APPROACHES TO THIS PROBLEM, BESIDES THE ONE YOU GAVE ME?

This question can be used to test the lawyer's judgment and to determine how flexible he is. By asking this question, the lawyer will have to identify other workable strategies and to explain why the one he is recommending is likely to produce satisfactory results.

If the other strategies seem appealing to you, pin the lawyer down as to precisely why he thinks one strategy is better than the next.

It may be that the lawyer's recommended strategy may be best suited to her personality and not necessarily the one best suited to solving the problem. In a breach of contract case, one lawyer may recommend that you fight everything your adversary tries to do and that you not give in an inch. You may feel that it makes more sense to settle the matter quickly instead of pouring money and energy into fighting over issues on which you may be willing to compromise. You may decide that this lawyer may not help you effectively accomplish your goal, which is to resolve your dispute quickly and with a minimum of expense and aggravation.

HOW DO YOU THINK MY ADVERSARY WILL BEHAVE?

There are many cases that ought to proceed in a rational, straightforward manner—but do not because the opposing party or law firm is difficult to deal with. To use divorce as an example once again: divorces are often emotionally charged. Some lawyers work to reduce conflict, others strive to develop an atmosphere that results in confrontation all the time. If your prospective lawyer knows the opposing lawyer's "style," it might give him an advantage when assisting you.

WHO WILL BE WORKING ON MY CASE?

The lawyer you're interviewing may make a great presentation. Next you have to find out whether he will actually be working on your case. Be blunt: ask who will do the work, what kinds of other matters the lawyer is working on, and how much time he will have after considering the complexity and urgency of your problem. If other lawyers in the firm are going to do the bulk of the work, then you want to know what their qualifications are.

In some firms, paralegals and/or secretaries may do a great deal of the routine matters, including returning your telephone calls. If anyone else will work on your matter, you should ask about their training and the manner in which their work is supervised.

WHAT TYPES OF FEE ARRANGEMENTS CAN I MAKE WITH YOU?

There are basically three types of fee arrangements you can make with attorneys:

1. Flat fee: An attorney may quote you a specific price for the matter to be handled. For instance, an attorney may quote you a flat fee for drafting a contract of sale of your boat for you.
2. Hourly fee: An attorney may charge you by the hour, charging you for the actual amount of time she or he worked on your matter.
3. Contingency fees: An attorney may charge you a percentage of the amount recovered on your behalf. A contingency fee arrangement is common in accident cases where you are seeking damages from someone else who has caused you injury.

Some states have laws prohibiting use of contingency fees on certain matters like criminal or divorce actions.

Sometimes, an attorney will combine two or more of the above when making fee arrangements. Your attorney may say that she will charge you on an hourly basis up to a certain maximum, and you will not have to pay anything extra after that maximum sum has been reached.

Attorneys may offer special reduced fees for their initial consultation with you (so you can meet them and decide whether you like them without having to incur a big bill). When you call to make an appointment, ask what she or he will charge for the initial visit, and how much time is covered by the special rate. An attorney may charge twenty-five dollars for the first half hour of an initial consultation, but after that charge an hourly rate of $100 per hour to handle your legal matter. So if your initial consultation with this attorney takes one hour, it will cost you seventy-five dollars (twenty-five for the first half hour, and fifty for the second).

HOW AND WHEN WILL YOUR FEE BE PAID?

In addition to asking the manner in which the fee will be computed, it's important to ask how and when payment will be expected. If you're quoted a flat fee, ask whether you must pay the whole thing up front, in installment payments at specific intervals, or whether you will be billed at the conclusion of the matter. If your attorney has quoted you a fee of $4,000 to handle your criminal matter, for example, must you pay the full amount up front, or can you pay $2,000 now and $2,000 before the trial?

If your attorney will be billing you on a hourly rate, he may ask you for a retainer to be paid up front against which he will draw money as he earns it by working on your matter. Ask whether a retainer will be required or whether you can pay as you go by having him bill you on a monthly basis.

If your attorney is billing you on a contingency basis, she'll ask you to sign a written retainer agreement outlining what those percentages may be (sometimes the percentages are tiered; for instance, 30 percent to the attorney for the first $50,000 recovered, 25 percent for the next $50,000 recovered, and 20 percent for the balance of the funds recovered on your behalf). In contingency fee cases, although you may not have to pay the attorney's fee if there is no recovery, you may still have to pay out-of-pocket costs incurred on your behalf for such things as court filing fees and testimony transcripts, so ask when these fees will be payable.

If you don't agree with an attorney's method of payment or feel the rates are too high, call another attorney and do some comparison shopping.

ARE OUT-OF-POCKET COSTS INCLUDED IN YOUR FEE?

In addition to asking what your attorney's fee will be, ask whether out-of-pocket costs are included in the fee quote or whether you'll be asked to pay for these separately.

Suppose you're starting a lawsuit. Ask whether the court filing fees are included in the attorney's fee quote or whether you will be expected to pay for them separately. (Depending upon the court and how the lawsuit progresses, costs can run to $500 or more.) If you're about to probate your mother's will in court, filing fees may be as much as $1,000 or higher in some areas. Once again, you need to ask whether these fees are included in the attorney's price quote.

Ask what the estimated out-of-pocket costs may be and

when you'll be expected to pay for them; often, attorneys will ask you to pay a sum up front that is estimated to cover most of the routine, anticipated out-of-pocket disbursements.

HOW MUCH WILL MY CASE COST IN TOTAL?

Unless you are quoted a flat fee for your case, including disbursements, you should be concerned about the ultimate cost of your matter. Unfortunately, it's often difficult to predict exactly what a case will cost. Not every case is routine, and sometimes it is impossible to estimate just how expensive a case will be until the case takes shape.

You may start what you think will be a simple lawsuit against a tenant who abandoned space he rented from you. However, after you serve your legal papers, you're advised that the tenant intends to impose a counterclaim against you for $100,000 damages for allegedly forcing him out of the rented space and demanding kickbacks from his business. He serves a notice to take your deposition before trial and a demand for all of your documents relating to your case, which include utility bills, tax bills, and expense bills for the six years he has been your tenant. What you thought would be an "open and shut" case has turned into a litigation war. So any fee that a lawyer originally quoted you, based on the original circumstances, may no longer be valid.

HOW DO I KNOW IF AN ATTORNEY'S FEE QUOTED TO ME IS FAIR?

Unless you have prior experience using lawyers for the kind of problem you are having now, it's hard to know whether a fee quoted to you is fair and reasonable. The quoted fee, which may seem totally beyond your reach, may in fact be fair and reasonable for your type of case.

What if you've been quoted a fee of $1,500 to cover the sale of your house, but one of your friends tells you that his attorney only charged $750. It could be that the sale of your house involves processing an application and attending a hearing for a building department variance to "legalize" a ten-year-old addition to your house—a problem your friend did not have. Unless you have similar circumstances to someone else, comparing your quoted fee with your relatives' and friends' may not be a good method of assessing its fairness.

The best way to find out whether a fee is fair is to talk to several lawyers, describe your matter in as much detail as possible, and ask them to provide you with an estimate.

IS THERE ANYTHING I CAN DO TO ASSIST YOU IN HANDLING MY CASE THAT COULD STREAMLINE YOUR WORK (AND REDUCE MY LEGAL FEES)?

This is an excellent question to ask to find out if the lawyer is interested in helping you save money. If he is, he'll suggest ways that you can prepare for meetings so that they'll take as little time as possible.

If you're looking for an attorney to discuss settlement of your mother's estate, the attorney should tell you to bring your mother's records to the first meeting so that she can prepare an inventory of the assets at that time, without having to schedule additional meetings to perform this task. Similarly, if you're looking for an attorney to discuss a possible divorce action against your husband on the grounds of cruel and unusual behavior, he should suggest that at the first meeting you bring a list of all the events upon which you base your case, as well as a list of your assets and liabilities so he can properly advise you of your prospects.

HOW DO I MONITOR THIS RELATIONSHIP?

Ask how long the lawyer expects the case to take until completion. Some matters are routine or can be done within a predictable time frame. A will can usually be drafted as soon as you have provided your attorney with the necessary information about your estate and intended beneficiaries; other cases are far more difficult to predict. Lawsuits often proceed slowly and require numerous court hearings—and can be delayed by crowded court calendars. Your lawyer should be willing to provide you with a periodic estimate of when he thinks your case will be resolved.

WILL I RECEIVE STATUS REPORTS ABOUT MY CASE?

Your attorney should voluntarily give you periodic updates on your matter. Ask whether she will give you copies of all correspondence and legal papers involved. Once you've chosen an attorney and begun working with her, you should ask whether the original strategy is working out successfully, whether events in your case suggest that a modification of strategy is needed, and whether the fees originally anticipated are on target.

Suppose your attorney told you your "no fault" divorce would take approximately six months to finish. Six months have passed and you're still not divorced. You are entitled to an explanation of why it's taking longer than anticipated and whether it's going to cost you extra because of the delay.

WHAT DO I DO IF I DON'T THINK THE RELATIONSHIP IS WORKING OUT?

Just like friendships and marriages, not all relationships with attorneys work out. Your attorney may be demanding and aggressive in handling your lawsuit when what you really wanted was someone who could act as a mediator to assist you in resolving your conflict. On the other hand, your real estate attorney may seem timid to you, and too quick to give in to demands made by the purchaser of your house. You may feel that he is not effectively representing your interests.

There is often a strong temptation to second guess your lawyers, particularly if things are not going as smoothly as anticipated. If you're dissatisfied because you think your case isn't going well, if you're having difficulty communicating with your attorney, or if fees and costs are not in line with your budget, you should discuss these matters with your attorney either in person or by telephone. The explanation you receive will either diminish your concerns or increase them.

WHAT DO I DO IF I THINK AN ATTORNEY HAS MISMANAGED MY CASE?

If you think an attorney has not handled your case properly, you should do the following (in this order!):

1. Ask the attorney why he or she has handled your case in that manner. Often, there are rules or procedures that must be followed or unusual circumstances that your attorney may not have fully explained to you.
2. Ask another attorney to evaluate what the first attorney has done. If you consult another attorney,

you may find that your original attorney's action was one of several legally permissible options and, in fact, the best choice under the circumstances.

Your local bar association can provide you with a list of attorneys specializing or concentrating in your area of the law, who often can provide insight into your situation. You may find out that your original attorney did the right thing after all. If not, proceed to step number three.

3. Consider a legal malpractice action. If an attorney has mismanaged your legal matter and caused you damage, you have the right to start a lawsuit against that attorney.

DO YOU MAINTAIN MALPRACTICE INSURANCE?

Most attorneys will maintain professional liability insurance that will protect them in the event they fail to perform competent legal services. If an attorney fails to handle your case properly, and if you bring a lawsuit against that attorney and he maintains malpractice insurance, there will be a source of funds, up to the face amount of the insurance policy, from which you can collect if you win. If not, you must look directly to the assets of the law firm or the individual attorney, and he may have legally put all of his assets in his wife's name before he started his law practice to protect against such a contingency—in which case you could be out of luck.

ARE THERE ANY REFERENCES YOU CAN GIVE ME TO CALL BEFORE I HIRE YOU?

Attorneys should be able to furnish you with names of people who can verify what kind of experience the attorney has and the character of the attorney. If the attorney you are interviewing seems startled or unnerved that you asked for references, don't be surprised; attorneys are almost never asked to provide references by their prospective clients.

Don't be surprised if your attorney says she'll have to get back to you with the names of references. If she wants to give you clients' names, she'll have to get their permission first, since under ethical rules she may not be permitted to disclose any clients' names to others without their express consent. Also, the attorney might be able to give you the names of nonclients, such as former employers, who can give you information as to the competence and integrity of the attorney, but she will probably want to get their permission first as well (as you would with any reference).

SECTION 2

CRIMES OF THE HEART: SMART QUESTIONS TO ASK ABOUT MARRIAGE, DIVORCE, AND CHILDREN

Getting married, having children, getting a divorce. It's sad that these three issues are connected in the same section. But it's a fact of real life, and a fact that may be difficult to face.

All three of these situations can be emotionally trying. Even the happy times, such as getting married or adopting a child, can produce a great deal of anxiety. And getting a divorce can be traumatic.

That's why asking questions is so important. You want to be sure you understand everything that is going on at times like these. You wouldn't want to adopt a child and find out six months later that your adoption hadn't gone through proper channels and you have to give up the child . . . . You don't want to get married and find out later that your spouse's first divorce wasn't legal . . . . And you certainly don't want to go through a divorce and then discover that you didn't get everything you need—and deserve!

It's important that you understand the why, what, and how of anything that so deeply affects your life (and your children's lives). A clear understanding of the law and your lawyer's action will let you know that these procedures are being done for you, not *to* you.

Asking questions also alleviates some of the fear and anxiety that often accompanies these procedures. It's not what we know that scares us; it's what we don't know. You make the unknown the known by asking questions.

Finally, asking questions forces the lawyer to relate to you, and lets her know that you expect to be actively involved in your legal affairs. Asking questions also lets her know that you want the best treatment you can possibly get. Make the lawyer think: think about what she's doing; think about what she's going to do; think about how she can best serve you.

I'M GETTING MARRIED IN A FEW MONTHS. IS A PREMARITAL AGREEMENT ADVISABLE?

Not necessarily. If you and your future spouse are young, have no children from prior relationships, have no assets to speak of, and have no complex business interests, you probably don't need a premarital agreement. But if you are middle-aged with children and many personal assets, you should consider such a document.

For instance, if you're marrying for the first time, but your spouse makes a lot less money than you do (and you want to be married for yourself, not your money!), you may wish to consider a premarital agreement that will separate the assets you had prior to marrying from the assets you acquire during the marriage. Are you and your future spouse going to live in a house you bought and paid for? Or are you going to use your inheritance money as the down payment on a house you will buy and hold in joint names? You may wish to consider a premarital agreement to cover these types of issues.

When children are involved, there are other issues to consider. If you have children from a prior marriage, you may wish them to inherit all of your money when you die. However, most states' laws provide that you can't cut a spouse out of your will unless you have an agreement to the contrary. A premarital agreement can state that your future spouse will waive his or her rights in favor of your children. If these or any other questions concern you, ask your lawyer to explain your rights to you before you get married.

WHO CAN LEGALLY PERFORM A MARRIAGE CEREMONY?

This depends on where you are. Each state and country has its own laws regarding who is legally permitted to perform marriage ceremonies.

On a ship in the middle of the Atlantic Ocean, the applicable law (which may be maritime law or the law of the country in which the ship is registered) would govern who is permitted to perform a marriage ceremony; the captain of the ship may be legally entitled to officiate.

On land, the laws of the local government prescribe who is entitled to perform a marriage ceremony. It is usually a local court judge or a person who is a member of a recognized religious order (such as a minister, priest, or rabbi).

IS THE MARRIAGE I GOT IN ANOTHER STATE (OR COUNTRY) LEGAL?

If the marriage was legally performed in the other state

or country, it will be legal in the state where you now live. A marriage ceremony performed in Mexico, for example, by a priest qualified under Mexican law to perform such duties, will be legal in the United States.

You should have received a legal certificate from the government in the place where your marriage ceremony was performed certifying that:

- the person who performed the ceremony was legally qualified to do so; and
- that you are legally married under the laws of that state or country.

If you do not have such a certificate in your possession, you might want to get a copy now instead of trying to get it later when you may need it in a hurry (e.g., in order to apply for death benefits after the sudden death of your spouse).

IS MY SPOUSE LEGALLY OBLIGATED TO SUPPORT ME?

It depends upon the circumstances. If you become the recipient of public assistance or care, your spouse may be legally obligated, to the extent he or she is able, to provide for your support.

On the other hand, if you had incurred debts in your name only, creditors will not ordinarily be able to charge your spouse with payment of that bill (unless the debt was for necessities such as food, clothing, or shelter, or unless there was a specific agreement with your spouse to be a co-obligor on that debt). Suppose you run up a large credit card bill. If your wife wants the right to charge items to your account, she will be asked to sign an agreement to the effect that she will be responsible for the entire bill if you fail to pay it.

I'M A MATURE WOMAN WHO HAS BEEN MARRIED FOR THIRTY YEARS. I'VE NEVER WORKED OUTSIDE THE HOME, NOR DO I HAVE ANY CREDIT IN MY NAME (EVERYTHING IS IN MY HUSBAND'S NAME). IS THERE ANYTHING I CAN DO NOW TO ESTABLISH CREDIT FOR MYSELF IN THE EVENT MY HUSBAND DIES OR I AM DIVORCED?

Contact your husband's creditors (credit card companies, utility companies, etc.) and ask that you be listed as a co-obligor on each of these accounts, and, if applicable, have a credit card issued in your name. (But remember, you are now responsible if your spouse runs up a bill and doesn't pay it!) You can also apply for credit (such as a department store credit card) in your own name.

If you're considering a major purchase, even if you have the ability to pay cash for the item, you may wish to take out a loan and make monthly payments on it over a period of time to establish a "track record" in your name. You might also ask your husband if some of your assets could be transferred into both of your names as joint owners (if he refuses, this might be a clue that a divorce proceeding is on his mind). An officer at your bank might also have suggestions for establishing credit in your own name.

MY MARRIAGE IS NOT VERY STABLE. IS THERE ANYTHING I CAN DO TODAY TO PREPARE MYSELF FOR THE POSSIBILITY OF DIVORCE?

Make sure you know about, and understand, your financial assets and responsibilities (as an individual and as a couple). If necessary, discuss your situation with a lawyer or financial adviser so that you can take whatever steps you need to take yourself. That doesn't mean you can be sneaky or play tricks with your assets. You can't hide your money by emptying out bank accounts or giving it away to relatives to try to prevent your spouse from getting at it. Normally, the court will force a spouse who has "cleaned out" the bank accounts to trace these funds when alimony, child support, and property settlement arrangements are being made.

For example, if you have a jointly held checking and savings account with your spouse, you may have the right to withdraw all the funds in the account and open an account in your own name using that money (this varies from state to state). However, if you do so in anticipation of a divorce, the court will still ask you what happened to these funds and will list these funds with your assets when determining how all of your holdings are to be divided.

HOW CAN I PREPARE TO MEET MY MATRIMONIAL ATTORNEY SO THAT WE CAN MAKE THE MOST EFFICIENT USE OF TIME WE SPEND AT OUR INITIAL MEETING?

If you have access to financial records—bank statements, tax returns, any documents that concern assets, liabilities, income, etc.—bring them with you when you meet your attorney. (If you don't have access to them, the court can compel your spouse to produce them at a later date.)

Many matrimonial attorneys ask their clients to prepare a written report including a history of the marriage—how long; how many children; what events led up to the decision to get a divorce, separation, etc.; a list of assets (both yours and your spouse's); employment history (yours and your spouse's); and any special requests that you want to negotiate for in the process. This helps clients give their attorney as much information as possible at the first meeting. It also helps the attorney organize your file and ask you questions based upon the information in the report.

For instance, if you want to divorce your husband

because of his acts of adultery, it would be helpful if you gave your attorney a list of the approximate dates and circumstances that led you to believe that your husband was having an extramarital affair (does he frequently "work" all night, and do you find hotel receipts in his pockets?). Or, if your wife is an alcoholic, you should include details in the report as to the frequency of drinking and the nature of her behavior when she is drinking (does she drink heavily all the time, and does she beat the children after she has a few drinks?).

The more information you can write down for your attorney, the less time you'll have to spend in your attorney's office and the more time your attorney will have to efficiently perform your legal work for you.

CAN I GET AN ANNULMENT INSTEAD OF A DIVORCE?

An annulment is a judicial pronouncement declaring a marriage invalid. There are many things that are grounds for annulment in most states, such as an underage party, an incestuous marriage, bigamy, and fraud.

There must be a valid reason to have a marriage annulled—you can't get an annulment just because you've been married a very short time (i.e., if you get married and decide a week later it was a big mistake). The circumstances under which you may obtain an annulment are usually very specific. Some examples of circumstances that may be grounds for annulment in your state are:

- You're an adopted child and you've married a person who you later find out is your natural brother.
- You've married a person who you now find out had a "quickie" Mexican divorce from her former spouse that is not legal in your state.

- You married a person who agreed to convert to your religious faith after the marriage but has now reneged on the promise.
- You married a person who had a false identification card showing that he or she was twenty-two but actually was only age fifteen.

I'VE HEARD PEOPLE SAY THEY ARE "LEGALLY SEPARATED." WHAT DOES THIS MEAN?

A separation is a legal status that falls somewhere between being married and being divorced. Although you are still legally married, a separation agreement or court order will define certain property rights and support rights for you and your spouse as if you were divorced.

SHOULD I GET A SEPARATION INSTEAD OF A DIVORCE?

You may wish to have a legal separation from your spouse before you get divorced for various reasons, including the possibility of reconciliation. You may be entitled to alimony and/or child support payments during the separation period. Ask your attorney to explain the advantages and disadvantages of each of your options.

Take a case where your spouse is trying to cope with a drug addiction problem. You find it impossible to live with her while she's still on drugs. However, you love her very much and you think once the rehabilitation process has progressed, you'll want to try to get back together. This situation may suggest having a formal separation first, to give you time to assess the severity of the problem and whether it can be worked out before considering something as final as a divorce.

Or your spouse's parent, who is terminally ill, has been

living with you and the strain of caring for him has become too much for you to handle. Although you love your spouse, you understand the needs of the near-death parent, and you think that you should move out until the parent is either transferred to a hospital or passes away.

In each of these scenarios, a separation might be a better alternative than a divorce, since these are hopefully temporary life crises that will eventually work themselves out.

IF I AM SEPARATED FROM MY SPOUSE, CAN I GET (OR WILL I HAVE TO PAY) ALIMONY?

You may be entitled to receive alimony if you're separated from your spouse. You and your spouse will either agree to the amount of the alimony, if any, or it will be decided by the court, after weighing all the facts and circumstances, as would also be the case in a divorce action. The alimony award may state that it is intended for the time of the separation only, and if there is a divorce later on, the terms of the award may be changed at that time.

For instance, if you're being separated from your spouse, one of you will probably be moving out of the marital residence and one of you will be staying. Either way, there will be costs of running a household, the same as if you were divorced. The alimony award in this case will help you defray the costs of the separate household.

IF I'M SEPARATED FROM MY SPOUSE AND I HAVE CUSTODY OF THE CHILDREN, WILL I RECEIVE CHILD SUPPORT?

If your spouse is the sole source of income for the family, he will be obligated to send you child support payments each week (month, etc.). If your spouse is the sole source of income for the family and also has custody of the children, you will probably not be asked to contribute to their support, at least initially, since you have no source of income. In a family where both parents have equal incomes, both the custodial parent and the other parent may be asked to contribute the support of the children.

WHAT IS A NO-FAULT DIVORCE?

In a divorce based on fault, you have to prove that your spouse provided you with grounds for ending the marriage, such as adultery, mental or physical cruelty, nonsupport, abandonment, or conviction of a felony. In a no-fault divorce, you only have to show that you are no longer able to live together as a couple.

If you and your spouse are just incompatible and have no other grounds for getting a divorce, you should consider a no-fault divorce (if it's available in your state).

In some states, a no-fault divorce is a two-step process which first requires that you live apart pursuant to a written separation agreement or court order for a year. After that, you may apply for a so-called no-fault divorce. A no-fault is not necessarily quick or easy, since even in a no-fault divorce there are still issues of alimony, child custody and support, and property settlement. Your no-fault divorce can still take a long time if you and your spouse cannot agree on all the details of the split-up.

WHAT IF ONE SPOUSE WANTS A DIVORCE AND THE OTHER ONE DOESN'T?

If your spouse is applying for a divorce on grounds other than a no-fault basis, such as abandonment, adultery, or cruel and inhuman treatment, she may be able to get a divorce whether you like it or not, provided she can prove the accusations that would support her case. If, however, she is applying for a no-fault type of divorce, you may have to consent before the divorce is actually granted, depending upon the laws in your state. So if you feel you and your spouse are incompatible, and you have no other legally sufficient reasons for asking for a divorce, you may have to enlist her cooperation to get a divorce.

I GOT A DIVORCE IN ANOTHER STATE. IS IT VALID IN THIS STATE WHICH IS MY NEW RESIDENCE?

Normally, if you get a valid divorce in another state (that is, the court had proper jurisdiction over the parties and the divorce was legally concluded in that state), your divorce will be valid in your new state. For instance, if both you and your spouse resided in the state where you got the divorce, both parties appeared and were represented by attorneys, and a divorce decree was made by that state's court, your divorce will be honored by all other states. However, if you went across the border to another state to get a quicker divorce, lied about being a resident of that state, your spouse never received valid notice of your divorce petition and never appeared in court, and you got a divorce by default (that is, no opposition), your spouse could challenge the decree. It makes sense to consult an attorney to make sure your divorce really does the job you want it to so you can be free to go on with your life.

I'VE HEARD THAT DIVORCE IS A LENGTHY PROCESS. CAN I GET ONE IN A FOREIGN COUNTRY (WHERE IT TAKES LESS TIME) AND WILL IT BE VALID HERE?

Depending upon the circumstances and upon the laws

of your state, a divorce obtained from a foreign country may or may not be honored.

If both you and your spouse moved to the foreign country and became residents, both appeared in the divorce action and were represented by attorneys, and the divorce action was legally concluded under the laws of the foreign country, your foreign divorce will probably be honored. However, if you flew to the foreign country without the knowledge or consent of your spouse and got a twenty-four-hour divorce from a divorce mill, this divorce will most likely not be honored by your local state.

The underlying theory behind divorce (and most legal proceedings) is that all parties must have notice and an opportunity to be heard, and if either or both of these requirements is missing, particularly in a divorce proceeding where substantial marital assets of personal and property rights are affected, the proceeding is considered invalid. Quicker is not necessarily better.

WHAT ARE CONSIDERED ASSETS OF A MARRIAGE?

Each thing that you own can be considered an asset of the marriage, including bank accounts, real estate, pension and profit-sharing plans, executive compensation plans, antiques, jewelry, cars, boats, furniture, money owed to you by others, stocks and bonds, cash, life insurance, annuities, etc., whether in your name alone or in joint name with your spouse, if accumulated during the marriage.

Assets you acquired before you were married may also be considered in this category. For this reason, you may want to sign a premarital agreement with your spouse as to how pre-acquired assets will be treated in the event of divorce. If you received a large inheritance from your first husband after his death, for instance, you may wish to provide that in the event of separation or divorce from your new spouse, this inheritance will be considered separate property not subject to marital division.

HOW WILL THE MARITAL ASSETS BE DIVIDED UP WHEN MY SPOUSE AND I GET DIVORCED?

As part of the divorce procedure, a division of the assets of the marriage will be made. You and your spouse can decide how these assets are to be divided up, or the court will decide for you if you are unable to do so.

It's usually better to work these things out in advance, since you may want to keep items of sentimental value. The antique vase your aunt gave you may be more important to you than the valuable painting you won at a raffle. Similarly, you may want to keep your boat, but you really don't care about the family automobile (which your spouse loves).

WHEN I GOT MARRIED, I BROUGHT A LOT OF ASSETS INTO THE FAMILY THAT ARE STILL IN MY OWN NAME (SUCH AS MONEY INHERITED FROM A RELATIVE). WILL THE COURT CONSIDER THIS IN MAKING A PROPERTY SETTLEMENT AWARD?

Assets accumulated before the marriage may be treated differently from assets accumulated during the marriage. If a premarital agreement specifically states these assets will be treated as yours alone, and if there is no fraud or overreaching (one party taking undue advantage of the other, such as one party being represented by an attorney and the other one not), the court will honor the agreement. If, however, you had no such agreement, the circumstances of the marriage will be taken into account when dividing the assets.

Suppose both you and your spouse inherited money from deceased relatives. You agreed that your spouse's money would be used as a down payment on a house and your money would stay in the bank. The court may treat the money still in the bank as a marital asset since your spouse's separate funds were used to purchase a jointly used asset. Make sure you give your attorney the exact details of your premarital circumstances so that she can make a fair assessment of how your assets should be divided.

WHAT WILL HAPPEN TO OUR MARITAL RESIDENCE IF WE ARE DIVORCED?

The disposition of the marital residence will be determined by the facts and circumstances of each case, as well as by local law. Many times a parent who has custody of the children will retain possession of the marital home until the children reach a certain age, at which time the home will be sold and the proceeds divided.

It may depend upon whose money purchased the house (were individual assets of one spouse from before the marriage used to make the purchase?). Even if the ownership of the home is in one spouse's name, it may be considered a joint asset for divorce purposes. For instance, it may be that before the marriage each prospective spouse owned a home, but after the marriage one home was sold and the other one kept as the family residence. Or the home may have been bought in the name of one spouse to protect it from claims of creditors of the other spouse. One spouse may "buy out" the interest of the other spouse, either by trading other assets for the share of the home or by obtaining a bank loan to pay cash to the spouse being bought out.

WHAT ARE THE TAX CONSEQUENCES OF MY DIVORCE (SEPA-RATION, OR ANNULMENT)?

Before you agree to the terms of a divorce settlement,

you should ask what the tax consequences of those actions will be. Alimony payments, for instance, are normally tax deductible by the payor and taxable to the recipient. However, child support payments are neither deductible by the payor nor taxable to the recipient.

Let's say that it takes $3,000 per month to run the marital home (including mortgage payment, taxes, utilities) and to support you and your two children. You may consider getting all this money in child support so you don't have to report it as income. However, child support will run out when the children reach a certain age, so you really want to weigh the pros and cons of such an arrangement. It may be better for you to receive the $3,000 in alimony payments, even though you have to pay taxes on the income. This may cover a longer period of time than the years during which you would be entitled to child support.

There are tax rules, however, which say that even if you call a payment alimony (or child support), if it really is another thing, the tax court will treat it as it's actually used. If your "alimony" payments are $3,000 per month but they happen to drop to $1,500 after your last child reaches age twenty-one, a portion of this payment may be considered child support and taxed as such. Be sure that you and your lawyer discuss tax ramifications of any cash or property disbursements.

WHO GETS CUSTODY OF MY CHILDREN IF MY SPOUSE AND I ARE DIVORCED?

One or both of you may be awarded custody. If you can't agree on child custody arrangements, the court will determine custody, taking into account "the best interest of the child." A full-time mother of two infant children might be awarded custody, for instance, since she has been their primary caretaker. However, if the children are ages fourteen and sixteen and get along well with both of their parents, a joint custody arrangement might be considered (assuming other circumstances are conducive to do so—for instance, that the parents both reside in the same school district and both have enough room in their homes for the children to stay for extended periods of time).

Most often custody of all the children in a family will be awarded to one parent. Under certain circumstances custody of one child could be awarded to the mother and custody of others awarded to the father. If two of the children are older and one is very young, it may be deemed best for the baby to reside with a parent who spends a lot of time a home (for instance, a father who does free-lance work from home as opposed to a mother who has a full-time job outside the home). In this case, the court may split custody of the children between the two parents.

I AM DETERMINED TO OBTAIN CUSTODY OF MY CHILDREN AFTER MY DIVORCE. WHAT CAN I DO, IF ANYTHING, TO ASSURE MYSELF THAT I (AND NOT MY SPOUSE) WILL GET CUSTODY OF THE CHILDREN?

There is probably no way you can guarantee that you will be awarded custody of your children. As discussed in the prior question, many of the factors considered by the court when awarding custody are already in place and cannot be altered—such as the ages of your children, your occupation, your spouse's occupation, and the current relationships you and your spouse have with your children.

There may be some things you can alter that can work in your favor. What is your current job situation? Do you have a highly demanding job that requires extensive out-of-town travel? If you change jobs to one that doesn't require travel and will get you home by 5:30 P.M. each evening, the court may look more favorably on your child custody request. Or, if you'll be the parent moving out of the marital residence, make sure that your new living arrangements will be conducive to living with children (such as having more than a temporary sofa bed in the living room for them to sleep on when they are with you).

IF I WANT CUSTODY OF MY CHILDREN, ARE THERE ANY FACTORS THAT COULD WORK AGAINST ME?

Depending upon the philosophies in your area, there are many factors that could be considered by the courts in disqualifying you as a custodial parent. In the past, mothers were almost always awarded custody of children. Today, many states have a public policy not to assume either parent is more fit than the other solely due to gender. However, a problem such as a history of drug or alcohol abuse or a history of neglect or child abuse would most certainly be given great consideration by the court. If one parent is a convicted felon, the court may prefer the other as custodial parent. Homosexuality of one parent may be a factor considered by the court. Living situation of a parent (are you now living with a lover?) may affect the court's decision. As discussed above, if you travel frequently in your job and would seldom be home (and you do not intend to change your job to a less-demanding one), the court might consider this a negative factor.

You can assume that if your spouse is as determined as you are to get sole custody of the children, all of your bad habits (relevant or not) will be paraded before the court in an attempt to show that he is the parent to whom custody should be awarded.

WHAT KIND OF VISITATION RIGHTS WILL I HAVE IF MY SPOUSE GETS CUSTODY OF OUR CHILDREN AFTER MY DIVORCE (SEPARATION, ANNULMENT)?

Your court order or agreement will set forth the general terms and conditions under which you will have visitation rights with your children. Your spouse may have custody of the children during the week, and you may have custody on the weekends. Or you may see your children every other weekend except for the summer, when you get custody of them. You may alternate holidays, or have another system for deciding who goes where on family occasions. It all depends on the family situation and the circumstances of the parents.

Suppose you're a teacher and have the summers off. It may make sense for you to have custody of the children during the months when you can spend a lot of time with them. Or, if you're a musician and work weekend nights, it may be better for you to take custody of the children during the week when your spouse works. Hopefully, no matter what your disagreements with your spouse, you'll be able to work out a child custody and visitation schedule that's good for both parents and children, with the help of your attorney.

MY SON'S FORMER WIFE JUST GOT CUSTODY OF THEIR CHILDREN. WHAT RIGHTS, IF ANY, DO I HAVE AS A GRAND-PARENT?

As a grandparent (or aunt or uncle), you may not automatically have the right to visitation of your grandchildren who live with your ex-daughter-in-law. Unless your state's law grants you visitation rights, you'll have to wait until a time when your son is entitled to visitation with his children and see them at that time.

However, even if there is no specific law granting you visitation rights, you may be able to get access to your grandchildren if you can convince the court you have a good reason for asking—such as if the father is now deceased, and you'll have no access to the children unless you're granted your own visitation rights.

IF I AM DIVORCED, MUST I PAY (OR WILL I RECEIVE) ALIMONY OR CHILD SUPPORT?

Payments of alimony and child support are dependent upon various factors, including length of the marriage, income of the spouses, and ages of the children, and vary from state to state.

For instance, if a woman has stopped her career to care for very young children, and she plans to continue to stay home full-time with them, the court may award her both alimony and child support. If an older woman whose children are grown up and moved out of the home is divorced, and she has never worked outside the home, the court may award her permanent or temporary alimony until she can find a job that will fully or partially support her.

If one parent has custody of the children, the other spouse may have to contribute to their support. For example, if the children reside with a mother who has little or no income, the father will most likely have to pay child support. But in the same situation, if the father has custody of the children, the mother will probably not be asked to contribute support money because of her limited financial means.

IF WE JUST LIVE TOGETHER WITHOUT GETTING MARRIED AND THEN WE SEPARATE, WILL I BE ENTITLED TO ALIMONY?

Unless the laws of your state provide for "common law" marriage (by reason of living together as if husband and wife even though no formal ceremony was performed), under most circumstances you will not be entitled to claim alimony payments.

You might, however, be entitled to certain property rights. If you can show that you paid for items that are now in the possession of your former companion, you may be able to sue to get possession of those items or get compensation for your financial investment. If you had children together, you will be entitled to claim child support if you have custody of the children.

HOW MUCH MONEY WILL I GET (OR HAVE TO PAY) FOR ALIMONY?

The court will look at such factors as the standard of living of the family, the length of the marriage, and the ability of the spouses to earn a living in making alimony awards. For instance, an older spouse who had had a lengthy marriage and an affluent lifestyle, and had raised children without holding an outside job, would probably receive a generous stipend for the rest of his or her unmarried life. A spouse of similar circumstances whose family income is lower might receive fewer dollars, but over the same duration of time. A short, childless marriage will probably result in little or no alimony payment. If both spouses work and earn equal or comparable salaries, neither may be asked to pay alimony to the other.

The divorce process can be devastating for a spouse who has never earned an income or has earned only a small income in comparison to her spouse. An alimony award is designed to soften the blows, if possible, and allow the less financially able spouse to piece together the rest of her life.

HOW MUCH MONEY WILL I GET (OR HAVE TO PAY) FOR CHILD SUPPORT?

The court will look at such factors as the standard of living of the household and the needs of the children when making child support awards. For instance, a family with an income of $20,000 per year will be evaluated differently than a family with an income of $2 million a year. While a parent whose income is low might be asked to make only moderate payments, a parent whose income is high will be asked to make much higher payments, and most likely cover many additional items.

For example, a wealthier parent may be asked to pay for the entire college education of his or her children, whereas a parent with lower income probably will not be asked to do so. Also, a wealthier parent may be asked to pay for such items as orthodontic work, summer camp, and other things that might be considered luxury items by a family of more limited means. A court will not force you to pay for items that are drastically beyond your ability to pay.

Similarly, the needs of each child must be taken into account when making an award of child support. For instance, if a child requires remedial help in reading in school and the family has been previously sending the child to a special tutor, the court will probably direct that payments for this tutoring continue, even if it is a minor hardship for the family. Or, if a child has a medical disability and requires special care or treatment, the court will direct this payment to continue even if that child will receive a disproportionate share of the child support payment.

WHAT ITEMS SHOULD I ASK FOR WHEN NEGOTIATING FOR ALIMONY?

When negotiating with your spouse for alimony payments, you may wish to ask for more than just money. Medical insurance coverage, for example, may be relatively expensive to purchase yourself, and your spouse may be able to continue coverage on you under his plan at little cost to him (his employer may already be providing family coverage).

Life insurance coverage is another item that may become important. If your spouse dies, you'll have no more source of funds for alimony payments. You should have your spouse secure a policy on his life on which you are both the owner of the policy and the designated beneficiary. (If you make the mistake of letting him be the owner of the policy, you may be surprised to find out later that he has changed his beneficiary or has borrowed against the cash value of the insurance policy, leaving less than the full face value of the policy to you after his death.)

A third item you'll want to obtain is attorney's fees to be paid by your spouse in the event she fails to live up to the terms of the divorce or separation agreement. Otherwise, if you have to enforce the divorce agreement, you won't be reimbursed for your attorney's fees.

You should also try and get a cost-of-living adjustment automatically built into your agreement so that you will have at least some protection against inflation whittling away at your source of income.

WHAT SHOULD I ASK FOR WHEN NEGOTIATING CHILD SUPPORT PAYMENTS?

You should consider some of the same items as discussed in negotiating for alimony, such as medical insurance coverage, life insurance coverage on your spouse's life (which can be owned by a life insurance trust, of which you can be the trustee for your children), attorney's fees in case of default, and cost-of-living adjustments.

In addition, you should consider items not covered by ordinary child support payments, such as (if appropriate) private school and/or college tuition, summer camp, dancing (singing, gymnastics, etc.) lessons, and other items that your children now enjoy or you anticipate that they may become involved in as they grow older. You don't want to have to return to court later on to try to add something you had not anticipated at the time you negotiated the arrangements.

WHEN NEGOTIATING FOR CHILD SUPPORT PAYMENTS, HOW CAN I ASSURE MYSELF THAT MY CHILDREN'S COLLEGE EDUCATION WILL BE TAKEN CARE OF?

Nowadays, with skyrocketing college costs, a simple promise in a divorce settlement to pay for a child's college education may not be enough. For instance, if your child is now three years old, it will be difficult to predict what college expenses will be in fifteen years. You may wish to negotiate to open up a bank or investment account under the Uniform Gift to Minors Act (if adopted by your state) in your child's name, with you named as trustee, into which your spouse must make periodic contributions. (Since you will be the trustee, you'll be getting the bank statements to verify that the contributions are being made as promised.)

There are also programs offered by certain colleges that allow you to prepay future tuition at their institutions (but they require the child to attend that particular college). If you're sure that your child will want to attend a particular college, this may be an option for you to consider. Ask your attorney to suggest some additional methods of making sure the money is available when your child is ready to attend college.

I UNDERSTAND THAT WHEN MY DIVORCE (OR SEPARATION) IS CONCLUDED, I WILL RECEIVE AN AWARD OF ALIMONY AND/OR CHILD SUPPORT. BUT HOW DO I SUPPORT MYSELF AND MY CHILDREN IN THE MEANTIME?

The court has the power to award you temporary alimony and/or child support while your court action is in progress. You should tell your attorney what your needs are and ask the court to award you temporary payments to tide you over until the matter is concluded. (The final amount of future payments will be determined in the agreement or divorce/separation decree.)

For example, the court can order your spouse to pay temporary alimony and child support for your three children, which will last until the divorce suit is ended, so that you'll have some income between now and the time of the settlement or award (which, in some cases, can be a long time).

WHAT HAPPENS TO MY ALIMONY AND CHILD SUPPORT ARRANGEMENTS IF I REMARRY?

Normally, alimony payments stop when the spouse receiving payment remarries. However, child support payments usually continue until the children attain the age or circumstances agreed to by the parties or directed by the court order.

IF MY SPOUSE DOESN'T REMARRY, HOW LONG A PERIOD OF TIME WILL I RECEIVE (OR HAVE TO PAY) ALIMONY PAYMENTS?

If nothing is said in the divorce (separation, or annulment) agreement or court order, alimony payments will continue during the lifetime of the recipient. Most awards provide that alimony payments stop if the recipient remarries or lives together with someone as husband and wife.

Individualized arrangements may be made whereby payments are temporarily higher to allow the other spouse time to train for a new career (for example, a former full-time mother who will later enter the job market) or to allow time to adjust in a new situation (such as living in a new location). Say your spouse is one year away from obtaining a teaching degree, which she has pursued part-time while raising your children. After that, she will be able to get a job as a teacher that will give her a means of support. You may wish to structure the payments so that they are higher until a reasonable period of time after she graduates, and then reduced after she (hopefully) secures a job as a teacher.

HOW LONG WILL I RECEIVE (OR HAVE TO MAKE) CHILD SUPPORT PAYMENTS?

Normally, child support payments continue until the children attain the age or circumstances agreed to by the parties or directed by the court order. The law specifies a minimum age at which time a parent is no longer legally bound to support his or her child (normally age eighteen or twenty-one); some states' laws also list other circumstances under which an obligation to support a child ceases (for instance, the marriage of a child). However, you can agree to any arrangement you wish, including support during years of extended education, such as medical school or law school.

When there are several children in the family, the agreement or court order should state the amount that child support payments will be reduced as each child reaches the specified age or contingency. For instance, if you have three children, ages three, six and nine, and you are receiving child support payments of $1,500 per month for all three, your document should state that upon the oldest child reaching the cutoff event, child support will be reduced to $1,000 per month, upon the middle child reaching the cutoff event, child support will be reduced to $500 per month, and upon the youngest child reaching the cutoff event, child support will be terminated.

CAN I STOP MAKING ALIMONY OR CHILD SUPPORT PAYMENTS IF MY SPOUSE DOES NOT ABIDE BY THE TERMS OF OUR DIVORCE (SEPARATION) AGREEMENT OR COURT ORDER?

You may be entitled to a temporary suspension of payments if your spouse violates a term of the agreement or court order, depending upon the circumstances. For instance, if your spouse refuses to let the children see you, you may be entitled to stop payments temporarily until he or she lets you see the children. However, you're not entitled to do this on your own; you must have a court order allowing you to suspend payments.

Suppose you had agreed to sell the marital residence when your youngest child became eighteen. Now the child is nineteen and you have willfully failed to put the house on the market. Your spouse may be able to get a court order suspending payments during the time you failed to live up to the agreement or court order.

Minor squabbling, however, is usually not enough to warrant cessation of payments, unless the minor incidents together can be considered a material breach of the agreement.

WHAT CONSTITUTES "BREAKING" OF A DIVORCE OR SEPARATION AGREEMENT?

As with any contract, breaking of a divorce or separation agreement occurs when there is a failure or a refusal to perform one or more of the "material" terms of the agreement. If your agreement burdens you with the obligation to pay alimony and/or child support, and you make no payments at all, this would be considered a breach of a material term. If, however, you were consistently one day late in making your payments, or if you missed a payment once a year but made it up during the next few months, this probably would not constitute a material breach of the agreement.

If you obtained custody of the children and failed to provide them with food, shelter, and clothing, this would be considered a breach of a material term of the agreement. If, however, you are supposed to return your children to your spouse by 7:00 P.M. on Sundays but you often return them between 7:30 P.M. and 8:00 P.M., this probably would not be construed as a material breach of the agreement.

MY SPOUSE, WHO STILL LIVES IN THE SAME STATE I DO, HAS FAILED TO PROVIDE ALIMONY PAYMENTS. WHAT CAN I DO?

If your state has appropriate laws, you may be able to go to court and get an order to force your spouse to make present and future alimony payments. You may be able to compel your spouse to make payments directly into court or face imprisonment for failing to obey a court order.

However, if there are past-due alimony payments that are owed, you may have to start a lawsuit against your spouse to collect what is owed, just as you would do with any other legal obligation.

So, if your spouse is regularly behind in making alimony payments, it may pay to get a court order compelling him to make present and future payments directly into court, instead of waiting until arrears accrue. If you must sue, it may pay to wait until there is a significant amount of money due, since you will not want the aggravation of starting lawsuits each month he misses a payment. However, the longer you wait, the less likely it may be for him to be able to come up with the money. It's best to consult your attorney as soon as arrears accrue so you can choose your best option for collection.

MY SPOUSE OWES ME PAST-DUE ALIMONY PAYMENTS BUT HE HAS NOW MOVED TO ANOTHER STATE. HOW CAN I COLLECT THE MONEY?

You may be able to get a judgment for the past-due sum in your own state and "convert" it to a judgment in the new state by bringing another court action in that state. You may also be able to start a lawsuit in the new state for the overdue alimony payments.

Suppose you live in New York and your spouse has gotten a new job in Chicago. Soon after your spouse moved, the alimony payments stopped. Your long-distance phone bill to your spouse's answering machine has increased without any additional payments being received by you. You can now start a lawsuit in New York and get a judgment for the arrears, and then start another (simplified) lawsuit in Illinois, where your spouse lives, to convert the judgment into an Illinois judgment. Once you have this judgment, you can enforce it just like any other judgement (such as by sending the sheriff to collect the money).

Or you can bring a lawsuit in Illinois directly. Ask your local attorney to establish a working relationship with a Chicago attorney so that your collection efforts can be coordinated. For instance, you may discover that although the court filing fees in Illinois are much less expensive than in New York, by starting your lawsuit in Illinois, it will ultimately be more costly, since you may have to fly there to make court appearances.

IT'S VERY EXPENSIVE FOR ME TO GO TO COURT EVERY TIME MY SPOUSE FALLS BEHIND IN ALIMONY PAYMENTS. ARE THERE ANY LESS EXPENSIVE ALTERNATIVES I CAN USE TO COLLECT THIS MONEY?

Plan ahead and insert a provision in your separation or divorce agreement stating that in the event of default in payment of alimony, you'll be entitled to attorney's fees. Then you'll have at least partial relief when you have to turn to the judicial system to collect past-due alimony payments (that is, if you ultimately collect the money you were awarded in your judgment).

You might also consider a small-claims court where procedures are simplified and geared toward people representing themselves; however, small-claims courts generally have a low monetary ceiling (for instance, $2,000) that you can recover in one court visit. Otherwise, you may not have other alternatives in your area.

MY SPOUSE, WHO STILL LIVES IN THE SAME STATE I DO, HAS STOPPED MAKING CHILD SUPPORT PAYMENTS. WHAT CAN I DO?

Most states have special child support enforcement procedures where you don't have to continually bring lawsuits against a spouse to keep the child support payments coming in. In many cases, you bring a petition into court in which you show that child support payments are not being made. The court will then set up a system whereby your spouse will make child support payments directly into the court, and the court will send them on to you. It may take a bit longer for you to receive payments, but it beats the alternative of no payments at all. If your spouse fails to make the payments into court, the court can apply appropriate sanctions, which may include imprisonment for contempt of court.

MY SPOUSE HAS MOVED TO ANOTHER STATE AND HAS NOW STOPPED MAKING CHILD SUPPORT PAYMENTS. WHAT CAN I DO?

To assist families in collecting child support payments from parents who have moved out of town, most states have adopted a uniform system of child support enforcement procedures. This means that a child support order from one state is automatically honored in another state. Sometimes, these systems are linked up by computer so that a child support order can almost instantaneously be sent to another state for enforcement.

For example, if you live in Texas and your spouse has moved to California, you may be able to go to your local Texas court and get a child support enforcement order that can then be automatically sent to California to be enforced. Ask your attorney whether your state has adopted the uniform-child-support-enforcement procedures and how this system can work for you.

HOW CAN I GET THE MONEY TO PAY MY BILLS WHILE I'M IN COURT FIGHTING WITH MY SPOUSE FOR PAYMENT OF ALIMONY AND CHILD SUPPORT?

Your attorney may be able to suggest state and local resources to contact who can advise you how to deal with your creditors while you are in litigation with your spouse. Credit counseling services might be helpful in suggesting methods of holding off your creditors until your spouse comes through with the cash. You might be able to get an emergency loan from a local resource group that supports families in need. If you're evicted from your apartment because you haven't had enough money to pay the rent, emergency housing may be available to you. As the rate of divorce has been rising, so have the number of support groups and agencies that can render assistance to families in time of need.

WHAT CAN I DO TO ASSURE MYSELF THAT MY ALIMONY OR CHILD SUPPORT PAYMENTS KEEP UP WITH THE COST OF LIVING?

Ask your attorney to negotiate a cost-of-living increase in your divorce or separation agreement to provide that your payments are increased periodically as the cost of living rises. Normally, a third-party source (such as the *Wall Street Journal*) will print a cost-of-living index that will contain a factor by which the cost of living has gone up over a particular period of time. For instance, if the index is 1.00 the day your divorce becomes final, and the next year (when your agreement says the payment amounts will be adjusted) the index is 1.04, your payments will be adjusted to account for this increase. If your weekly payment was $100 in the above example, your weekly payment would be increased to $104 because of the four percent increase in the cost of living that year. (This is a simplified example for the sake of clarity; your actual increase formula may be more complicated.)

Your spouse may not want to have such an arrangement, but may instead ask for an increase linked to her actual pay raises over a particular year. The problem with this arrangement is that unless a third-party standard is chosen to measure the increases, there may be future disputes between you and she as to the actual amount of the increase. What if she chooses to take an unpaid leave of absence from her job? Your spouse may argue that her pay scale has now gone down to zero and therefore no alimony payments are due to you.

WHAT IF I DID NOT NEGOTIATE A COST-OF-LIVING INCREASE IN MY ALIMONY OR SUPPORT PAYMENTS? CAN I GO TO COURT AND GET AN INCREASE IN MY PAYMENTS?

In some areas, so long as no extraordinary changes have occurred in your life (for example, a child has become seriously ill and now needs you at home full-time, so you can no longer work at an outside job), you cannot get an upward modification of your alimony and child support payments. A mere increase in the cost of living without any other factors normally is not enough to warrant a modification. That's why it's so important for you (and your matrimonial attorney at the time) to ask for a cost-of-living increase when conducting your original divorce negotiations.

However, if you feel burdened by unanticipated circumstances, ask your attorney whether you may be entitled to petition for an increase in payments.

IF I HAVE AN INCOME OF MY OWN, WILL I BE PENALIZED IN TERMS OF MY ELIGIBILITY TO RECEIVE ALIMONY PAYMENTS FROM MY SPOUSE?

The purpose of alimony payments is to provide income to a spouse in a reasonable manner so that one spouse does not live in poverty while the other enjoys a lavish style of life. The former spouse of a successful surgeon who makes a substantial income should not have to apply for welfare payments because she cannot meet her financial obligations. If both spouses have equal or nearly equal incomes, the court may not award alimony at all. If you and your spouse are both research scientists with equal incomes, neither of you will probably get an award of alimony payments. So in that sense, if you have an income, you may be "penalized" in terms of your eligibility to receive alimony payments from your spouse.

WHAT IF YOUR SPOUSE EARNS A HIGH SALARY AND YOU ONLY HAVE A MODERATE INCOME?

In that case, the court may direct that your spouse make alimony payments to you, depending upon the differential between the salaries. For instance, if your spouse is a business executive making $100,000 a year and you are a student making $10,000 a year, it's likely that the court will order your spouse to pay you alimony to partially close the gap between the two incomes, at least until you have finished your degree and gained additional earning potential.

If your spouse makes $100,000 a year as a plumber and you make $80,000 a year as a public relations manager, the court may consider the incomes substantially equal and award you little or no alimony.

MY SPOUSE HAS OFFERED TO GIVE ME THE HOUSE IN EXCHANGE FOR REDUCED ALIMONY PAYMENTS. IS THIS A GOOD DEAL?

Although getting the house (a substantial asset) may seem at first glance to be a good deal, before rushing to say yes, you should consider several different factors.

First, does the house have existing mortgages, and can you afford the monthly mortgage payments? Remember, you must have sufficient monthly income to pay not only the mortgage, but real-estate taxes, maintenance, and utilities.

Second, do any of your spouse's creditors have judgments or liens against the property that you will have to pay off? If your spouse has run up substantial debts, once the house has been transferred into your name, your spouse's creditors may be coming after you.

Third, does the present value of the future alimony payments (that is, the value today of future money, discounted for inflation, cost of living, and interest value) you are thinking of trading away, approximate the present value of the house (excluding liens)? If the discounted value of the prospective future alimony payments exceeds the present equity in the house, it may not be such a good deal after all. If you wait for the alimony, you may be getting substantially more money than if you get the house. You or your attorney can hire an actuary to calculate these values for you.

RIGHT AFTER WE GOT DIVORCED, MY HUSBAND QUIT HIS JOB AND STARTED A NEW BUSINESS, WHICH IS NOW BRINGING IN TWICE THE INCOME HE USED TO MAKE AT HIS OLD JOB. CAN I GO BACK TO COURT TO GET HIGHER ALIMONY PAYMENTS NOW THAT HE IS MAKING SUBSTANTIALLY MORE MONEY?

The mere fact that your husband is making more money now than before you were married may not, by itself, be sufficient grounds for you to petition the court for more alimony. The standard of living you had during the marriage will be a significant factor in determining the amount of the alimony award. Just because your spouse is now better off, through upturn in business, inheritance, or winnings, may not automatically entitle you to more alimony.

Say your husband is a construction worker making a weekly income of $900. He wins a state lottery that pays him an additional $1,100 per week, for a total of $2,000 per week. You're probably not entitled to a portion of his lucky break. However, if you can prove that you and he bought the ticket together before the marriage broke up, using family money, you might convince the court that you're entitled to a piece of the action.

I JUST LOST MY JOB. WHAT HAPPENS IF I CAN'T MAKE MY ALIMONY OR CHILD SUPPORT PAYMENTS?

If there is an unforeseen and unreasonable change in your circumstances, you may be entitled to a modification of your alimony and/or child support arrangements. However, a temporary or minor change of financial condition may not merit a modification of alimony and/or child support.

If you've lost your job and there are many similar positions available in your area, and you don't expect to be out of work for a long period of time, you're probably not a good candidate for a modification in your alimony and/or child support payments. However, if you were severely and permanently disabled in an automobile accident and were unable to return to the type of work you performed before the crash, the court will probably grant you a reduction of your alimony and/or child support payments, as well as a possible suspension of these payments while you're unable to work.

If you've been out of work for a while and forced to get a job that pays substantially less than your last job, you may be entitled to a permanent or temporary reduction of your payments.

MY SPOUSE HAS VOLUNTARILY QUIT HIS JOB. NOW HE'S APPLYING TO THE COURT TO DECREASE MY ALIMONY PAYMENTS BECAUSE HE'S OUT OF WORK (HE'S CLAIMING "JOB BURNOUT"). WILL HE BE ABLE TO VOLUNTARILY DECREASE HIS INCOME SO THAT HE DOESN'T HAVE TO PAY ME ALIMONY?

Unless there is a compelling reason to be out of work (such as layoffs or plant closings), the courts will not look favorably upon someone who quits his job for the apparent purpose of avoiding alimony payments. The courts consider heavily the earning potential of the spouse both during the marriage and afterward to determine whether or not an application for a decrease in alimony payments is legitimate. While a spouse may be out of work temporarily and the court may respond by giving a temporary alimony decrease, his or her overall employment prospects will be the determining factor for a permanent decrease.

MY SPOUSE OWNS HIS OWN BUSINESS WHICH ALWAYS PRODUCED A GOOD INCOME WHILE WE WERE MARRIED. JUST BEFORE HE STARTED DIVORCE PROCEEDINGS, THE BUSINESS BEGAN TO HAVE A DOWNTURN. HE'S NOW LOOKING TO ESTABLISH A LEVEL OF ALIMONY PAYMENTS COMMENSURATE WITH THE ALLEGED DOWNTURN IN THE BUSINESS. HOW CAN I FIND OUT WHETHER HE IS JUST REDUCING INCOME DURING THE DIVORCE SETTLEMENT PERIOD TO SET AN ARTIFICIALLY LOW ALIMONY FIGURE?

You and your attorney are allowed to examine all the books and records of the business. You can also question your spouse and his employees under oath to determine whether there really is a downturn in business or whether your spouse is fixing the books to show a lower income. If you can prove that he has purposely reduced the income of the business in anticipation of the divorce proceeding, you'll probably be able to get higher alimony payments than he is proposing.

If, however, there's a recession in his industry (or the area in general), there may be little you can do to establish a higher alimony payment. Similarly, if your spouse has lost interest in the business and does not choose to pursue it, there's not much you can do to force him to work harder to turn the business around.

I WORKED HARD TO SEND MY WIFE THROUGH DENTISTRY SCHOOL, WORKING TWO JOBS AND TAKING CARE OF THE CHILDREN. OUR PLAN WAS THAT WHEN SHE GRADUATED, I WOULD AGAIN PURSUE MY CAREER AS A FREE-LANCE WRITER. AFTER SHE GRADUATED, SHE STARTED A DENTAL PRACTICE WHICH HAS A MODEST INCOME NOW, BUT WHICH HAS THE POTENTIAL FOR MUCH MORE. SHE NOW WANTS A DIVORCE. CAN I CLAIM A PERCENTAGE OF HER PRESENT (AND FUTURE) PRACTICE IN OUR DIVORCE PROPERTY SETTLEMENT, BECAUSE OF ALL THE WORK I DID TO SEND HER THROUGH SCHOOL?

In the past, professional practices were not considered "property" for the purposes of making a marital property settlement. Today, more and more courts are allowing claims against present and future earnings of professionals in situations where one spouse put the other through school.

So, if you decide after finishing medical school that you want to divorce your spouse (before you start to make any money), you may find out that the court will award your spouse, who worked hard to put you through school, a percentage of your present and future earnings in that practice.

I JUST FOUND OUT THAT IN ANTICIPATION OF OUR UPCOMING DIVORCE, MY SPOUSE SECRETED ASSETS INTO JOINT BANK ACCOUNTS WITH HER BROTHERS AND SISTERS (WHO NEVER LIKED ME ANYHOW). NOW THAT WE'RE IN THE MIDDLE OF DIVORCE PROCEEDINGS, THE SIBLINGS CLAIM THAT IT IS THEIR MONEY. HOW CAN I GET ACCESS TO THESE FUNDS?

You'll have to prove that it was your spouse's money and not your in-laws'. You may still have a hard time physically getting the money back, particularly if the siblings already withdrew the money and spent it. They may claim it was a gift, and present proof that there was a scheme of gift-giving, unrelated to the upcoming divorce, particularly if your spouse had a good income and a generous philosophy.

MY SPOUSE HAS FILED A PETITION FOR BANKRUPTCY. HOW WILL THIS AFFECT MY ALIMONY AND CHILD SUPPORT PAYMENTS?

If your spouse files a petition for bankruptcy, he or she will still have the obligation to pay alimony and child support, including arrears. The federal bankruptcy law provides that a debtor can not have his alimony and child support obligations canceled ("discharged"), so he or she must still make all current and past-due payments. However, you may be legally delayed in getting past-due payments if your spouse gets a court order allowing him or her to do so, for instance, under a payout plan. (See the section on bankruptcy for more information.)

I WAS ABOUT TO START A LAWSUIT AGAINST MY WIFE FOR DIVORCE, BUT SHE STARTED ONE FIRST. WHAT HAPPENS NOW?

If your spouse sues you for divorce first, you have the right to counterclaim against your spouse for a divorce on whatever grounds you might have. For instance, if your spouse has started a lawsuit against you for a divorce and is alleging adultery, you have the right to counterclaim for a divorce on the grounds of abandonment. In your counterclaim you can ask for alimony and child support, too, just as if you had started the lawsuit first. You don't lose any legal rights if your spouse happens to start the lawsuit first; you may just lose a tactical advantage by not being the first one to strike.

IF I GO TO COURT AND GET A DIVORCE, WILL MY COURT RECORDS BE AVAILABLE FOR PUBLIC INSPECTION SO THAT ALL OF MY "DIRTY LAUNDRY" WILL BE AIRED BEFORE ANYBODY WHO WANTS TO LOOK AT IT?

Unlike most other court records, matrimonial proceedings (divorce, separation, annulment, child support, etc.) are not usually available for public inspection. Only the parties themselves or their attorneys can normally get access to these records.

Suppose you just went through a lengthy divorce proceeding with extensive testimony concerning the adulterous habits of your spouse (with your spouse countering with attempts to demonstrate that you physically abused her). The testimony transcripts and other court papers that may contain similar accusations or proof will probably not be made available to the public. However, you should ask your attorney about this, and whether there is any preventive action you must take to make sure these records do not come under the public eye.

IF I HAVE TO GO TO A COURT HEARING ON MY DIVORCE (SEPARATION, ANNULMENT), WILL THE PUBLIC BE ALLOWED TO ATTEND?

In most cases, your family-related court matter will not be open to the public, or you can request that the hearing be closed to the public. This is to protect the privacy of the parties. For example, if you're trying to get your marriage annulled because your wife failed to disclose to you before you were married that she's unable to have children, and you intend to offer extensive testimony from her doctor concerning her condition and her knowledge of the condition, she will most likely be able to exclude the general public (including the press) from the proceedings.

IF MY SPOUSE AND I ARE HAVING DIFFICULTIES IN OUR MARRIAGE, ARE THERE ANY ADVANTAGES TO REMAINING LEGALLY MARRIED INSTEAD OF GETTING SEPARATED OR DIVORCED?

By remaining married, you'll probably be better off financially than if you are separated or divorced. You may be able to maintain the same standard of living (assuming your spouse continues to support the household by providing income and/or services). You'll save money by maintaining only one household (one mortgage/rent payment, one set of utilities, etc.). However, the emotional sacrifices may not be worth the financial savings.

For instance, your spouse may be seeing a lover and flaunting the relationship in front of you. This may be too much for you to bear. However, if you and your spouse have developed different interests over the years and now lead happy but independent lives, staying legally married may be the choice for you.

I HAVE HEARD THAT DIVORCE MEDIATION IS AN ALTERNATIVE TO STARTING A LAWSUIT TO GET A DIVORCE. IS MEDIATION A VIABLE ALTERNATIVE?

If you and your spouse agree, divorce mediation may be an alternative forum in which you can work out your differences. A trained mediator will listen to both sides and suggest alternatives that can result in an agreement suitable to both spouses. It may be a cheaper, quicker, and less aggravating method of negotiating an agreement if both spouses are willing to abandon polarized positions in favor of meeting the other party halfway.

For instance, if you and your spouse can agree on everything except custody of the children, a mediator might be able to suggest solutions you haven't considered and bring the matter to a mutually satisfactory conclusion. If, instead, you take the dispute to the courtroom, the judge will be allowed to pick the solution, which may make neither of you happy.

ARE BOTH PARENTS OF A CHILD LEGALLY RESPONSIBLE FOR PROVIDING SUPPORT TO THAT CHILD?

Many states have laws stating that both parents are jointly and sense responsible for the support of their children. That is, each parent has an obligation to support his or her child and can be held responsible for the child's full support if the other parent fails to live up to his or her obligation.

If your spouse, who had custody of your children, takes all the child support money and skips town, leaving the children behind, you are legally responsible for support of your children. (You can try to catch up with your spouse to recover the money if you can locate him or her.) Or, if your child needs institutional care, both you and your spouse are legally responsible for paying the bills. If your spouse fails to pay, the institution could make a claim against you for the entire amount of the bill (even though you and your spouse had a deal to pay the bills on a fifty-fifty basis).

IS MY NEW HUSBAND OBLIGATED TO SUPPORT MY CHILDREN FROM A PREVIOUS MARRIAGE?

Under normal circumstances, your new husband is not obligated to support your children from a previous marriage. You and your former spouse have that obligation. However, your local law may provide that if the parents are unable to support the children, and the children become recipients of public assistance, the stepfather may become obligated to provide support to minor-age stepchildren. So, if your former husband is unable to supply support payments to your children and your children become the recipients of public assistance payments, and your new husband has the means to support them, he may become obligated to support them.

MY SPOUSE AND I WANT TO ADOPT A CHILD. WHAT ARE THE LEGAL PROCEDURES INVOLVED?

You'll have to bring a formal adoption petition in court. The natural mother and possibly the natural father may have to sign consent forms releasing their parental rights. There may be one or several court appearances to be made, where you're asked to testify about the circumstances of the adoption and your fitness to be parents.

Once you've located a child you want to adopt, your attorney files a petition in court for you and your spouse to become adoptive parents. The natural mother, or both parents, if required, sign consent forms. The court may schedule a hearing at which you and your spouse are requested to appear, as well as the natural mother or both natural parents. If the hearing is successfully concluded, you may be well on your way to becoming adoptive parents.

WHAT IF THE NATURAL MOTHER OR PARENTS CHANGE THEIR MIND AND DECIDE NOT TO CONSENT TO THE ADOPTION OF THEIR CHILD AFTER ALL THE PAPERS HAVE BEEN SIGNED?

Normally, after the consent forms are signed by the natural mother or parents, there is a waiting period during which they have the right to change their minds about the adoption procedure. After the waiting period is concluded, they may be asked to sign additional forms stating that they still want to go through with the adoption. Until the waiting period is concluded and all necessary papers have been signed, there is no guarantee that the natural parents will not change their minds. However, once the waiting period is finished and all paperwork duly executed, an adoption order will become final.

ONCE THE ADOPTION PAPERS BECOME FINALIZED, DO THE NATURAL PARENTS HAVE ANY RIGHTS CONCERNING THE CHILD, SUCH AS VISITATION RIGHTS?

Once the adoption proceedings have been finalized, the natural parents have, voluntarily, given up all of their rights concerning the adopted child. This means that they will not have the right to visit the child, unless you consent, nor will they have the right to go to court to set aside the adoption, unless there is a showing of fraud or undue influence on your part.

If the natural parents are duped into thinking that they were only signing foster home papers instead of permanent adoption papers, they have grounds to set aside the adoption. Or, if you tell the natural parents that you're childless and that's why you want to adopt, when really you've been convicted of child abuse and your own child was taken away, the natural parents have grounds for reopening the adoption proceedings. Other than extreme examples such as this, adoption proceedings are permanent, the records are sealed and are not made available to the public.

When the adopted child becomes an adult, he or she may have the right to petition the court to see the records.

I AM A SINGLE ADULT, AND I WANT TO ADOPT A CHILD. IS THIS LEGALLY POSSIBLE?

Generally, any competent and qualified adult may adopt a child. Usually, if there is an adoption agency involved, the agency will screen applicants for prospective parents whom they believe will be the best for the child. If given a choice, most agencies prefer a traditional family setting (husband and wife) to a single-parent situation. However, if you're willing to adopt a "hard to place" child, such as one with a physical or emotional handicap, you may have a good chance of becoming a parent even though you're single.

Even in a private adoption setting where you're dealing directly with the natural mother or parents, you might find it hard to convince the natural mother that placing her child with a single parent is better than placing him or her with a married couple. Once the parties to the adoption agree, the courts will not usually interfere with the arrangement unless it appears that it is not in the best interest of the child, or there has been fraud, illegality, or undue influence.

For instance, if the court finds that the single parent, desperate to adopt a child, has promised the natural mother a substantial cash payment after the adoption is finalized ("baby selling"), the court will deny the adoption petition.

WE ARE A LESBIAN COUPLE AND WE WANT TO ADOPT A CHILD. CAN WE DO SO?

Most states do not recognize a gay or lesbian couple as a legal entity for the purposes of adopting a child. However, the law is changing constantly and you should ask your attorney to advise you if the laws change in your area. It might be possible for one of the parties to adopt the child as a single parent, but the other partner would have no legal rights as a parent. This could be a problem in cases where parental consent is required (for example, medical treatment of a minor, marriage of a minor, etc.). The other partner would be without legal authority to act. Similarly, if the couple splits up, the nonadopting partner would have no rights to custody or visitation of the child.

I HAVE BEEN UNABLE TO FIND A CHILD IN THIS COUNTRY TO ADOPT, SO I WANT TO ADOPT A CHILD FROM ANOTHER COUNTRY. WILL THE FOREIGN ADOPTION BE LEGAL HERE?

If a valid adoption procedure was done in another country, in which the rights of all of the parties were sufficiently protected, the foreign adoption would be honored in this country.

For example, if you contacted an adoption agency in Colombia, all the legal proceedings were completed there, each of the parties was represented by an attorney, and you returned with all necessary certified translations of the adoption documents, you should have no problem in having others honor the foreign adoption proceedings.

I HAVE ADOPTED A CHILD WHO IS NOW (A YEAR LATER) SUFFERING FROM AN INHERITED DEGENERATIVE BRAIN DISEASE. THIS CHILD WILL NOW REQUIRE FULL-TIME, AT-HOME CARE THAT I CANNOT FINANCIALLY OR EMOTIONALLY PROVIDE. ALTHOUGH IT TEARS ME APART, I'M NO LONGER ABLE TO CARE FOR THIS CHILD. CAN I "UNADOPT" THIS CHILD?

Each state will have its own cases and laws that may or may not deal with the issue of rescinding an adoption. Generally, so long as there was no intentional hiding of a child's physical or mental condition from the adoptive parents, the child now is the legal ward of the adoptive parents, and such a problem would be handled in the same way you would for a natural child.

So, if you adopted a child who later developed a serious emotional personality disorder, you, as the parent, are now responsible for the care and well-being of the child, and you must manage the situation as best you can, with the possible assistance of state, federal, and local child welfare agencies.

MY WIFE AND I WANT TO HAVE A FAMILY, BUT WE HAVE DISCOVERED THAT MY WIFE CANNOT BEAR A CHILD. A FRIEND OF HERS HAS VOLUNTEERED TO BEAR A CHILD FOR US, USING MY SPERM AS DONOR. ARE SURROGATE MOTHERHOOD CONTRACTS LEGAL IN MY STATE?

Despite the recent publicity about surrogate parenthood, not all states have enacted laws that regulate this area. Before entering into any surrogate parenthood arrangement, you should ask your attorney whether such contracts will be honored in your state, or whether there may be other states where such an arrangement can be entered into.

The legal problems that exist are many, including the fact that the sperm donor's wife will want to adopt the child of the surrogate mother, and the birth mother will have to, in the process, surrender all of her parental rights. What if the surrogate mother changes her mind? Are payments to the surrogate mother for carrying the baby illegal? If the birth mother does not consent to the adoption, the situation will be similar to a divorce in which one of the parties has remarried. There will be issues of child support, custody, and visitation of both the birth mother and possibly the relatives of the child (such as grandparents).

MY HUSBAND IS UNABLE TO HAVE CHILDREN. WE WENT TO A SPERM BANK AND I WAS ARTIFICIALLY INSEMINATED WITH THE SPERM OF A MAN WHO I WAS TOLD HAD SIMILAR PHYSICAL CHARACTERISTICS TO MY HUSBAND. HOWEVER, WHEN THE BABY WAS BORN, THE CHILD WAS OF A DIFFERENT RACE THAN MY HUSBAND AND I. ALTHOUGH I LOVE MY BABY, I BELIEVE THE SPERM BANK EITHER NEGLIGENTLY OR INTENTIONALLY USED THE WRONG SPERM. WHAT RECOURSE DO I HAVE AGAINST THE SPERM BANK?

When you enter into a contract with someone, you are entitled to get what you bargained for. If you were intentionally deceived or if the sperm bank was negligent by inseminating you with the wrong sperm, you may be entitled to money damages against them. Your local laws will determine how these matters are handled in your area. For instance, if the sperm bank failed to screen an applicant for a genetic defect for which a simple test is available, you may be entitled to damages in the amount of the additional care the disabled child will require over his lifetime. If a child conceived by artificial insemination develops a mental disorder that was not evident in the family tree of the sperm donor, however, it is unlikely that you could recover damages from the sperm bank or the donor.

I AM AN UNMARRIED MOTHER, AND I WANT TO HAVE THE FATHER OF THE CHILD LEGALLY BOUND TO PROVIDE CHILD SUPPORT TO MY CHILD. HOW DO I GO ABOUT DOING THIS?

Most states have laws that authorize a court proceeding to determine if a man is the legal father of a child, even if that person is not initially listed on the birth certificate as the natural father. Normally, there is a time period within which such a proceeding must be started, so it is wise to consult an attorney to find out how long you have to make up your mind.

If the natural father is certified by the court proceeding, he'll be responsible for child support payments until the child is of legal age, but he'll also become entitled to child custody or visitation rights. Some fathers bring the proceeding themselves so they can gain these rights.

I THINK MY EIGHTEEN-YEAR-OLD SON IS USING DRUGS. CAN I USE DRUG-TESTING DEVICES TO FIND OUT WHETHER HE IS, EITHER BY TESTING THE ITEMS IN HIS ROOM OR HAVING HIM UNDERGO A CHEMICAL TEST (URINE, BLOOD, OR HAIR FOLLICLE)?

The issue of whether a parent has the right to "invade" the privacy of an adult (or a minor) child's room or body to test for illegal substances is one of concern for many parents.

You may have strong suspicions that your child is a drug user (you notice a drastic change in your child's behavior, sudden lack of interest in school, change of friends, etc.), but when you confront your child directly, she denies any involvement in drugs. You could probably go to her room while she is out to search for evidence of drug use or to find a hair follicle to send to your local laboratory for testing. However, you'll need her voluntary cooperation or a legally enforceable method of obtaining a urine sample or blood sample from her. Whether or not you are acting legally will be determined by your local laws. It's a good idea to ask your attorney before taking any action.

MY SPOUSE PHYSICALLY (OR MENTALLY) ABUSES ME. WHAT CAN I DO TO HAVE THIS STOPPED?

Although for many years cases of spouse abuse were virtually ignored by the legal system, there are now legal remedies available that can help to curb this problem in most jurisdictions. You may be entitled to an order of protection, which prohibits your spouse (or other person) from coming near you or your home. A valid order of protection (which you and your attorney must apply to the court to get) is enforceable by the police, so that if the prohibited person tries to come near you, he or she can be arrested and charged with violation of the court order.

MY SPOUSE (OR OTHER PERSON) PHYSICALLY ABUSES MY CHILDREN. WHAT CAN I DO TO HAVE THIS STOPPED?

Traditionally, child abusers are universally scorned by all, and the police have seldom been reluctant to arrest and charge an abuser. Unlike spousal abuse, when minor

children are abused, the state often steps in to protect
children from being hurt by others. Similar to spousal
abuse, you may be entitled to obtain an order of protection prohibiting the violating person from coming within
the vicinity of the abused child, either at home, at school,
or in other locations.

A convicted child abuser parent might also lose certain parental rights, such as the rights to visitation or
custody of his or her children. There are also social agencies available to help you and your attorney in seeking
remedies for your problem.

I KNOW FOR A FACT THAT MY NEIGHBORS PHYSICALLY ABUSE THEIR CHILDREN. DO I HAVE A LEGAL DUTY TO REPORT THEM TO THE POLICE OR A SOCIAL SERVICE AGENCY?

Some people are legally obligated to report cases of suspected child abuse to the appropriate authorities. For
instance, if you are a physician or social worker, you may be
mandated by law to report any suspected cases of child
neglect or abuse. Let's say you're an emergency-room worker in a local hospital and a child is brought in to you with
several broken bones and multiple bruises, and the parents
state that the child was hurt "playing." If your state's laws
so provide, you must report this case to the police if you
suspect that the parents' story is questionable.

In many states, you have no legal obligation to report
possible incidents of child abuse or neglect if you're not in
one of the special categories. So, if you're a neighbor or a
friend and suspect that someone you know is harming
their children, you may have no legal duty to turn them in.

AM I RESPONSIBLE FOR DAMAGE DONE TO A NEIGHBOR'S PROPERTY BY MY MINOR-AGE CHILD?

If your minor child destroys someone else's property, you may be responsible for making restitution to your neighbor for the damage done. For instance, if your child defaces the front of your neighbor's house with spray paint, you may become responsible for picking up the bill for a new paint job for the front of your neighbor's house.

Just as parents have the obligation of supporting children until they reach the age of majority, parents can be held responsible for the civil damages their children incur. However, under criminal laws, parents cannot incur criminal liability for acts of their minor children. That means that if your neighbors decide to call the police after your child spray-paints the house, and your child is charged with a juvenile crime, you will not be prosecuted merely because you are the parent of that child—unless you somehow participated in the crime, perhaps by sitting and watching in your lawn chair, sipping lemonade and encouraging your child to do the evil deed.

I BELIEVE THAT MY FOURTEEN-YEAR-OLD DAUGHTER IS OBTAINING CIGARETTES AND HAS, AGAINST MY WISHES, TAKEN UP A SMOKING HABIT. IS THERE ANYTHING I CAN LEGALLY DO TO PREVENT HER FROM OBTAINING THESE CIGARETTES?

As a parent of a minor-age child, you have certain rights in dealing with your child. Many states have a minimum age, under which a vendor cannot legally sell certain things, such as cigarettes. If you find out that a vendor is selling a regulated product to your underage child, you may be able to have the vendor arrested.

MY CHILD IS FIFTEEN YEARS OLD AND WANTS TO GET MARRIED. CAN SHE DO SO WITHOUT MY PERMISSION?

The laws of your state will specify the minimum age someone is allowed to be married and whether she must get your written permission before doing so. For instance, your state's laws may provide that no one under the age of sixteen may be married under any circumstances, with or without parental permission. These laws may also provide that once she turns sixteen, if she has your permission, she can be married. Also stated in the law will be the age at which anyone may be married, such as age eighteen. If your child is nineteen but is dreadfully immature and you despise her fiancé, there may not be much you can do to prevent the marriage.

THE PUBLIC SCHOOL THAT MY SON ATTENDS JUST SENT HIM HOME WITH A NOTE STATING THAT HE WILL NOT BE ALLOWED TO RETURN TO SCHOOL UNTIL HE CUTS HIS HAIR TO CONFORM WITH A NEW "DRESS CODE" THAT THE SCHOOL HAS ENACTED. SINCE THIS IS A PUBLIC SCHOOL, CAN'T I FORCE THE SCHOOL TO EDUCATE MY CHILD?

In some communities, schools have tried to regulate the appearance of the students. In a group where all the parents are in agreement with the standards set by the school (for instance, a private school), no problem is presented. However, where a publicly funded school arbitrarily demands that all students meet the standards of a dress code, legal issues may be present.

Parents have successfully brought lawsuits to force public schools to educate their children. A parent may argue that since local law usually mandates that children attend school until they have reached a certain age, it also means that schools have an obligation to provide free education to all students, regardless of their personal habits. Another argument might be that since public schools must provide public education and access for mentally and physically handicapped students, shouldn't they also be forced to educate the ones who choose to dress differently? Your attorney should be able to advise you which of these arguments has been successful in your area.

I DO NOT WANT TO SEND MY CHILD TO PUBLIC SCHOOL, AND I CAN'T AFFORD PRIVATE SCHOOL. CAN I LEGALLY EDUCATE MY CHILD AT HOME?

If you cooperate with your local and state education authorities in meeting a minimum standard of education for your child, you should be able to successfully educate your child at home. School systems may already have policies in place that specify minimum standards to be achieved and standardized tests to be given periodically to measure a student's progress.

For children who require extreme medical care and can't attend normal classes at school, alternate teaching and testing guidelines may have already been developed. You may be able to use these same guidelines in planning your own child's education. However, if you yourself have little education, you may have a difficult time convincing local and state educators that you have the ability to be an effective teacher.

SECTION 3

HOME SWEET HOME: SMART QUESTIONS TO ASK ABOUT BUYING, SELLING, OR RENTING YOURS

We may be living in the age of information, but we're also living in the age of transportation. Every day it gets easier and easier to move from one place to another.

That makes our choices about where we live much broader. We don't have to live within a few blocks of where we work, or around the corner from our parents or siblings. One person working for XYZ corporation might live in an apartment a bus ride away from headquarters, while another XYZ employee commutes from a farm out in the country, and a third takes the train in from a condo in the suburbs.

We all appreciate the freedom of choice we have nowadays. But along with this freedom comes confusion. Especially now, with the country in a recession and the housing market in a downhill slump. How can you protect yourself and make sure that you're getting the best possible deal—whatever choice you make?

By asking questions. By making sure you understand exactly what your rights are, and by letting your lawyer know you want everything explained to you clearly and completely.

A few weeks ago I heard a very intelligent, but very busy doctor talking about a condominium he was about to purchase. When I asked him if he would be allowed to do some remodeling he had been discussing, he answered, "I don't know. I never asked about that. I guess my lawyer will find out." How will the lawyer know it's important if the doctor never even questions him about it?

Many people have the attitude that "my lawyer will take care of all the details." Lawyers do the best they can, but they are not mind readers. Ask questions about the things that are important to you—that way the lawyer knows they're important, too.

Whether you're buying a home, selling, or renting, you need to know you're getting the best deal possible. Don't be afraid to ask for something if you feel you're entitled to it. If you're wrong, your lawyer can explain why and perhaps offer an alternative you (or he) may not have thought of before.

WHAT'S THE DIFFERENCE BETWEEN OWNING A HOUSE, CONDOMINIUM, COOPERATIVE APARTMENT ("CO-OP"), OR TIME-SHARE APARTMENT?

Be it ever so humble, there's no place like a home of your own. Not so long ago, if you were looking for a place to hang your hat there were two main options open to you: You could rent an apartment or you could buy a house. Now there are many more choices available,

including those listed below. The basic differences are as
follows:

1. A house: You probably own both the building and
   the land underneath, unless you rent the land on a
   long-term lease and own only the building above it.
   You must make all repairs and/or alterations, and
   you're responsible for maintenance.

2. A condominium: You own the inside of your unit
   only, plus a portion of the common areas (e.g.,
   underlying land and recreational areas). You cannot make any alterations to the outside of your
   unit, and you may be required to get the condominium association's permission to make any alterations to the inside of your unit. All repairs and
   maintenance inside your unit must be done by you;
   all repairs and maintenance to the outside of your
   unit should be done by the condominium association.

3. A cooperative apartment ("co-op"): You do not own
   the building or the land outright; rather you own
   shares in a corporation that owns the land and
   building, together with the right to occupy your
   apartment. You cannot make any alterations to
   your apartment without permission from the corporation's board. Your lease may require that all
   repairs be made by the corporation (although they
   may charge you separately for repairs made inside
   the apartment).

4. A time-share apartment: You don't own the land or
   the building, but only a right to occupy the unit for
   a specified period of time each year (e.g., the first
   week of each year). You can't make any alterations,
   inside or out; the management company will make
   all interior and exterior repairs and be responsible
   for all maintenance.

I'M TIRED OF RENTING MY APARTMENT BECAUSE OF ALL MY LANDLORD'S RESTRICTIONS. IF I BUY A HOME, WILL I STILL RUN INTO RULES, REGULATIONS, AND RESTRICTIONS?

Just because you're buying a new home, that doesn't mean you can always do whatever you want with it. There may be restrictions in the land records or in the rules of the association that oversees the complex. The homeowners' association, condominium board, or cooperative apartment board may restrict or prohibit certain activities, such as regulating the number or kind of pets you may have. For example, your condominium rules may prohibit any more than two pets in one unit, and may limit the kind of pets to domesticated animals such as dogs, cats, fish, and birds.

Before you sign any contract, make sure that any activity you love (e.g., gardening or outdoor barbecuing) is not prohibited. Ask if there are any restrictions, and make sure you see a copy of them. If you don't like the restrictions, don't sign the contract. Once you've signed and closed the deal, you have to follow the rules laid out in the contract.

I'VE SIGNED A CONTRACT TO SELL MY COOPERATIVE APARTMENT. MY LEASE PROVIDES THAT BEFORE I DO, THE PROSPECTIVE BUYER MUST BE INTERVIEWED AND APPROVED BY THE CO-OP BOARD. AT THE INTERVIEW, THE BOARD TOLD MY PROSPECTIVE PURCHASER THAT THEY WOULDN'T APPROVE HER SINCE HER SALARY DIDN'T MEET THEIR ESTABLISHED MINIMUM LEVEL. CAN THEY REJECT HER ON THE BASIS OF HER INCOME?

Under the law as it stands in many areas, so long as a co-op apartment board doesn't discriminate in one of the "suspect" categories, such as on the basis of sex, race, color, creed, or national origin, they can make up any combination of requirements they wish for prospective tenants. They may be able to provide that they will allow only college graduates in the apartment complex. They can also decide that a prospective buyer just doesn't "fit in" personality-wise with the existing group of tenants. All of the existing tenants may hate classical music, and they may have agreed that they will allow no concert pianists as tenants in the building. Or they can decide that if you haven't made at least one box office hit movie, you will not be permitted to purchase an apartment. Although it doesn't always seem fair or reasonable (who knows how many purchasers you may have to find before they will like one?), they are legally permitted to exclude others on almost any basis.

MY NEIGHBORS IN MY CONDOMINIUM COMPLEX HAVE TOLD ME THAT THEY DON'T LIKE MY PROSPECTIVE PUR-CHASER BECAUSE SHE DRIVES A MOTORCYCLE. THEY SAY THEY'LL SUE ME UNLESS I CANCEL THE CONTRACT. DO THEY HAVE THE RIGHT TO DO THIS?

A condominium is considered real estate (versus a cooperative apartment, where all you own is shares in the corporation that owns the building). Under the law you can sell to whomever you please without review by your neighbors or anyone else.

An underlying theory of real estate in this country is free alienability of property—that is, the ability to sell real estate without restriction. This gives you the right to sell to people who may not be well liked by your soon-to-be-ex-neighbors. On the flip side, if your neighbors don't like the new owner, they're free to sell their condominiums and move elsewhere.

WHAT EXPENSES WILL I HAVE TO PAY TO BUY/SELL MY HOME?

There's no way to make a general estimate of what your expenses will be. They vary depending on where you live and upon the type of home (house, cooperative apartment, etc.) you're buying or selling.

If you're buying a house, for example, you may have to pay your bank a fee to process your mortgage application, a fee to appraise the house you want to purchase, "points" (a percentage of the principal amount of the mortgage you are borrowing, typically 2 to 3 percent), fees to obtain a credit report on you as a prospective borrower, fees to your local land records department to record the deed and mortgage in their records, and title insurance fees to insure the transaction.

The seller of that same house may have to pay a real estate broker's commission (if the house was sold with the assistance of a broker), transfer tax (based upon the sale price of the house), and document recording fees to satisfy an existing mortgage on the property.

Who pays which of these expenses may vary from state to state. In some areas, the buyer instead of the seller will pay transfer tax on the property, or sometimes both the buyer and the seller may have to pay transfer tax.

Ask your attorney what expenses are usually involved in the type of transaction you're considering. He or she should be able to furnish you with a fairly accurate estimate.

WHAT LEGAL PRECAUTIONS SHOULD I TAKE BEFORE I SELL MY HOME?

First, have a lien search made against your home to check for unsatisfied liens. Suppose you signed a home improvement loan fifteen years ago and paid it off five years ago. Unbeknownst to you it was really a mortgage; now the contractor is nowhere to be found to sign a release. You must now start a lawsuit to get the mortgage discharged in the land records. This will possibly delay your closing date, so it is prudent to do a lien search in advance so that your closing is not held up because you're unable to get a release for this mortgage.

You should also check the local building department records to see that all of the structures on your land are "legal." What if the extension built onto your home by the previous owner was never "signed off" (inspected by your local building department and issued a certificate of completion)? Your contract with the buyer could require you to clear up the problem. Since the buyer's bank will probably not schedule a closing date until a certificate of completion is obtained for the extension, you'll be doing yourself a favor by investigating this possibility in advance so that your sale is not held up by a paperwork snarl in trying to "legalize" a part of your home.

Your purchaser will probably insist upon a clause in your contract of sale stating that the roof does not leak, and that the plumbing, heating, and electrical systems and the appliances are in good working order. It's a good idea to have any necessary repairs made in advance (these repairs may also enhance the salability of your home, since evidence of water damage may turn off a prospective buyer).

I'M ABOUT TO SELL MY HOUSE. DO I NEED A FORMAL CERTIFICATE OF COMPLETION FOR THE DECK I BUILT ON THE BACK OF MY HOUSE?

Whether your deck requires a formal certificate depends upon the size and location of the deck and your local building department regulations. Some municipalities do not require a certificate of completion for a deck unless it's more than six inches above the ground or more than a certain number of square feet. On the other hand, some areas require that formal application and inspections be made for all decks, regardless of how small or low to the ground. You should call your local building department in advance of selling your home to find out what the requirements are in your area.

If you're buying a house, be sure that you ask if any additions or changes have been made and that they are all legally certified by the building department.

ARE THERE ANY SPECIAL LAWS IN THIS AREA THAT I NEED TO COMPLY WITH BEFORE I SELL THE HOUSE?

In some jurisdictions, you're required by law to have working smoke alarms installed in your home as of your closing date. If you don't have them, it's better to install them in advance, instead of waiting for the last minute (and hoping your contractor will show up to do the work). Ask your attorney this question as soon as you consider selling. That way you'll be prepared to sell as soon as you find a buyer.

I'M CLOSING ON THE SALE OF MY HOUSE NEXT WEEK. BEFORE I COULD CALL MY OIL COMPANY TO TELL THEM NOT TO MAKE THEIR ANNUAL FUEL OIL DELIVERY, THEY CAME AND FILLED UP MY THOUSAND-GALLON OIL TANK, AND I HAD TO PAY THE BILL. WILL I BE REIMBURSED BY THE BUYER FOR THIS EXPENSE?

Normally, your written contract of sale will specify a list of items that will be apportioned between the buyer and the seller as of the closing date. Such items may include real-estate taxes, fuel oil, rents (if part of the property is being rented to a tenant by you), existing transferrable fire and casualty insurance contracts, interest on existing mortgages (if the current mortgage on the property is being taken over by you), water charges, and sewer rents.

In the preceding example, you'll be reimbursed by the buyer for the amount of oil in your tank as of the closing date if your contract stated that this was an item of apportionment. Similarly, if you had paid the real estate taxes on the property for the entire year up front, your attorney will compute the amount of money to be reimbursed to you, based upon the tax year of the taxes that were paid (the tax year is not always the calendar year).

Your purchaser may be able to take over the existing mortgage on your house. If your mortgage payment is due on the first of the month and you close on the fifteenth of that month, you'll owe the purchaser a half month's interest. When the purchaser makes his mortgage payment next month, he will then only be paying his fair share of the interest from the day he took title to the property.

IF I SELL MY HOUSE, HOW LONG DO I HAVE TO BUY ANOTHER HOUSE BEFORE I HAVE TO PAY FEDERAL CAPITAL GAINS TAX ON THE SALE?

Under current law, you have two years to reinvest your money in another house to avoid paying federal capital gains tax on the profit you made on the sale of your house.

SHOULD BOTH MY SPOUSE AND I SIGN A CONTRACT OF SALE FOR REAL ESTATE?

If the house is owned by both you and your spouse, both of you should sign a contract to sell real estate, otherwise the contract will be void, since all of the persons who own the house must sign the contract of sale.

On the flip side, if you and your spouse are purchasing real estate, both may want to sign the contract so that you both own the property after closing of title. That way, if one spouse dies, the other would automatically own the property.

WHAT IS A BINDER? HOW IS IT DIFFERENT FROM A REAL ESTATE CONTRACT?

A binder is a document a real-estate agent may ask you to sign when you make an offer to purchase a house. It should only authorize your real-estate agent to communicate your bid to the seller on the home you are buying, and it should state that a contract of sale for the home will be executed at a later date if the seller accepts your offer. With a binder, you can change your mind and cancel the deal if you have not yet signed a contract of sale.

When your real-estate agent asks you to sign a document labeled a "binder," check carefully to make sure it is not really a contract of sale. If it does not specify that a contract of sale is to be signed at a later date, you are signing a contract and you can be bound by its terms.

WHEN I MADE MY FINAL INSPECTION BEFORE BUYING A HOME, ALL OF THE SYSTEMS IN THE HOUSE AS WELL AS THE APPLIANCES WERE IN GOOD WORKING ORDER. HOWEVER, A WEEK AFTER THE CLOSING, THE MOTOR IN THE FURNACE "DIED." DO I HAVE ANY RECOURSE AGAINST THE SELLER?

Depending upon the laws of your state, you may be entitled to reimbursement from the seller for things that go wrong after the closing. Some states have laws protecting buyers of newly constructed homes that provide a guarantee period after the closing during which the seller is responsible for defective construction work or faulty appliances. If something doesn't work properly during the warranty period, the builder will have to come in and correct or replace the defective item, so long as the problem was not the fault of the new home-owner. On the other hand, your state's laws may contain no protection for you if you're buying a used house, so if an appliance breaks or a plumbing pipe bursts after the closing, you may have no recourse against the seller.

Sellers who are not compelled by law to provide warranties will usually refuse to give any. However, if you discover that the seller willfully concealed a defect, such as a leaky roof, you may be entitled to start a lawsuit against him.

AT THE SAME FINAL INSPECTION OF THE HOME I'M PURCHASING, I NOTICED THAT THE HEATING ELEMENT IN THE STOVE WASN'T WORKING. AM I ENTITLED TO A NEW STOVE?

Most purchasers will insist upon a clause in the contract that states that all appliances included as part of the house will be in "good working order" (that is, perform the job they are supposed to do, such as a washing machine that properly washes clothes) as of the date of closing.

Most sellers' attorneys add the caveat that if the appliances are not in good working order, the seller may either repair or replace the appliance, at the seller's option. Since the cost to repair the stove will most likely be much less expensive than the replacement cost of the stove, your seller will probably opt to have the stove repaired.

DURING THE FINAL INSPECTION, I ALSO NOTICED THAT ALL OF THE SHRUBBERY IN THE FRONT YARD HAD BEEN REMOVED. AM I ENTITLED TO A REDUCTION TO THE PURCHASE PRICE BECAUSE OF THIS?

Your written contract of sale should contain a list of all items that are deemed to be included (or excluded) from the property you are purchasing. For instance, your contract should specify whether such items as plumbing, heating, lighting, and cooking fixtures, bathroom and kitchen cabinets, shades, screens, awnings, mailboxes, pumps, shrubbery, fencing, toolsheds, appliances, and carpeting will or will not be included in the sale. Some people attach sentimental value to things such as plants (they may have been a present from a now-deceased relative), so they will specifically exclude them from the contract of sale.

In the above example, you should check your contract of sale to see whether you are entitled to the shrubbery. If it was included in the contract of sale, you'll be entitled to be reimbursed at closing for the value of the shrubbery that was removed. If the shrubbery was not included in your contract of sale, you may be out of luck.

MY FRIEND TOLD ME THAT AT HER REAL-ESTATE CLOSING THE BANK REQUIRED HER TO PAY SIX MONTHS' WORTH OF REAL-ESTATE TAXES ON THE NEW HOUSE UP FRONT, EVEN THOUGH THEY WERE COLLECTING MONEY TO PAY THE REAL-ESTATE TAXES IN HER MONTHLY MORTGAGE PAYMENT. WHY DID THIS HAPPEN?

In many cases a bank will require you to pay an additional amount each month in your mortgage payment as escrow (that is, money put aside in a special account) for future real-estate taxes. The bank does this so they can

pay the real-estate taxes directly and avoid the possibility of your municipality putting your property up for sale
if real-estate taxes are not paid. (If the municipality puts
the property up for tax sale, this may cut off the rights of
your bank as holder of your mortgage.)

However, the bank wants to be covered in case the
taxes are due before the bank gets enough money in your
escrow account. Therefore, they require you to pay what
they estimate to be the amount of the deficiency up front
so they don't have to reach into their own pockets to
advance the money.

WHAT HAPPENS IF THE HOME IS DESTROYED BETWEEN THE DATE OF CONTRACT AND THE DATE OF CLOSING?

If your contract doesn't contain a specific clause about
this possibility, you must look to local law to determine
the rights of the parties. Under general contract law, if
the house is completely destroyed, the parties may be
entitled to cancel the contract, since the object of the
contract is no longer in existence.

However, an additional question in real-estate sales is
who must pay for repair or replacement costs under circumstances where fire or catastrophe has damaged or
destroyed the premises. Normally, a seller must pay up
until the date the buyer either takes possession of the
property or completes the purchase, whichever is soon-
er. So, if a fire partially destroyed the home a week before
the closing and the home was still in the possession of
the seller, the seller would bear the risk of loss, and if the
buyer insisted, the seller would be obligated to rebuild
the house and complete the sale.

If the buyer had taken possession of the house several
days before the closing but had accidentally left the fire-
place going, which caused a fire, the purchaser would

have to pay. The seller could force the buyer to go on closing and still pay the full purchase price for the house, without any reimbursement for the fire damage. (For this reason, if you're a buyer and intend to take possession of your house ahead of the closing date, your attorney will insist that you purchase homeowner's insurance effective from the date you take possession. That way you'll be covered in the event of fire or other catastrophe.)

IS THERE ANY TYPE OF INSURANCE I CAN PURCHASE TO ASSURE ME THAT I WILL NOT HAVE BIG, SURPRISE BILLS TO REPLACE MAJOR ITEMS IN AN OLDER HOUSE AFTER I HAVE PURCHASED IT?

A relatively new insurance product, known as home warranty insurance, is now becoming available to buyers of previously owned homes. This could mean that you will not have to pay out large chunks of money if an appliance breaks down or a mechanical system fails after a closing. If you have purchased your home through a real-estate broker, she probably has information as to how you can purchase this type of insurance.

The theory behind such insurance is that you pay a premium, in exchange for which the insurance company will repair or replace a broken or defective item at little or no cost to you (there may be a deductible sum you must pay first) during the covered period. If you're buying an older house (let's say forty years old), which still has its original heating system and other old appliances, you may find that home warranty insurance coverage is worthwhile. However, if the house you're buying is eight years old, purchasing such insurance may not be a good investment, since the mechanical systems and the appliances in your home probably still have a few good years left in them.

WHAT IS TITLE INSURANCE, AND SHOULD I PURCHASE IT WHEN I BUY MY NEW HOME?

Title insurance protects you, as a homeowner, from someone making a claim of title to, or a lien against, your home due to acts that occurred prior to the date you purchased it. There is a one-time charge for this insurance and it stays in effect for as long as you own your home. All competent attorneys will insist that you purchase title insurance when you purchase a house or condominium; title insurance may also be advisable when purchasing a cooperative apartment or a time-share apartment.

If you're getting a mortgage from a bank, the bank will also insist that you purchase title insurance in its favor, to protect its interest as holder of your mortgage (the bank wants to be assured that there are no liens that are superior to its mortgage loan).

Before the closing, your attorney will order a title insurance report, which will verify that the person with whom you signed the contract of sale really does own his house (and not his father, who died five years ago). The report will determine whether the tax bills are paid up to date, and the exact amount of the current taxes. It will also tell you if there are any liens, such as mortgages or judgments, against the property that should be paid off by the seller at or before the closing date of your purchase.

The protection you get from title insurance is this: If someone tries to make a claim of ownership or a lien interest in your home, your title insurance company will have to resolve such a claim without you having to hire your own attorney to solve the problem. If any lien has to be paid off, they will do so, up to the face amount of your title insurance policy.

MY MORTGAGE BROKER HAS SUGGESTED THAT I PURCHASE "MORTGAGE" INSURANCE COVERAGE. WHAT IS MORTGAGE INSURANCE, AND SHOULD I PURCHASE IT?

Mortgage insurance is really a type of life insurance policy in the (ever-declining) amount of your unpaid mortgage on your home. What "mortgage" insurance does for you is guarantee that if you die leaving an unpaid balance on the mortgage loan against your home, this unpaid balance will be paid in full upon your death. It is an optional type of insurance sold by some banks and mortgage companies. If you prefer the security of knowing that if you die, your mortgage will automatically be paid off, you should consider purchasing this type of insurance. However, a generally less expensive term-life-insurance policy can accomplish the same goal. Your life insurance agent can advise you, if this is your concern, what the best deal is for you.

AFTER I'VE SIGNED A CONTRACT TO PURCHASE REAL ESTATE, CAN I CANCEL THE DEAL IF SOMETHING HAPPENS, SUCH AS IF I CAN'T GET A MORTGAGE LOAN?

Your contract of sale may contain clauses that provide that upon the occurrence of certain events, you or the other party may cancel the contract.

Your contract may provide that you can cancel the deal if you can't obtain a mortgage commitment within a specified period of time. Or, if your seller cannot produce "clear title" to the property (for instance, there are liens on the property in excess of the purchase price and the seller will not be able to pay them all off with the proceeds of the sale), the contract may provide that the seller can decline to go through with the sale.

You should ask your attorney what the normal contingency clauses are in your area. If you have any special conditions you want in the contract, have your attorney add them in before you sign it.

I HAVE BEEN OUT OF WORK AND I AM BEHIND IN MY MORTGAGE PAYMENTS. I JUST RECEIVED A LETTER FROM THE BANK STATING THAT IF I DON'T BRING MY PAYMENTS UP TO DATE, THEY'LL FORECLOSE ON THE MORTGAGE. WHAT ARE MY RIGHTS?

If you read the terms of your mortgage loan agreement, it will most likely state that if you default in performance of any of the terms of the mortgage loan agreement, including making your monthly mortgage payments, the lender will be entitled to pursue certain remedies, including starting a foreclosure action. If you ignore these notices from your bank and fail to bring your mortgage payments up to date, you can be sure that you will soon be served with legal papers to start a foreclosure action.

If you have a temporary problem, including being out of work, you should contact the bank and try to make arrangements with them; often, you can arrange to make payments over time without the bank resorting to its foreclosure option. Call your lender and explain any extenuating circumstances. Even though the lender technically has the right to foreclose as soon as you fall behind in your payments, if you're cooperative, the lender may choose not to use that option. After all, the lender is in the business of lending money and earning interest on that money, and is not particularly interested in foreclosing on your home unless there's no other choice.

AFTER MAKING PAYMENT ARRANGEMENTS WITH MY BANK TO BRING MY PAST-DUE MORTGAGE PAYMENTS UP TO DATE, I COULD NOT KEEP UP THE PAYMENTS, AND THEY DID START A FORECLOSURE ACTION. WILL I LOSE MY HOME?

If you do not settle your case beforehand (by paying up all of the arrears and court costs, usually including attorneys' fees as per your mortgage loan agreement) and a judgment of foreclosure is entered, you will lose title to your home. The judgment of foreclosure will appoint a referee as the new owner of your home. The referee will set up a date for a foreclosure sale, at which time anyone will have the right to bid on your house to buy it. (The minimum bid will usually be the amount of the mortgage you owe.) At the date for the foreclosure sale, the referee will sell your home to the highest bidder. The lender usually will bid the minimum bid, but depending upon the amount of the loan balance and the value of the property, others may make higher bids.

For instance, if your loan balance is only $15,000 but the value of your home is $100,000, there will most likely be investors who will be willing to bid over the $15,000 minimum but less than the $100,000 market value to get a bargain price on your home. If your home is sold for an amount in excess of your loan obligation, you'll be entitled to the excess money, less expenses of the foreclosure sale (such as auctioneer's expenses). In the above example, if a bidder purchased your home for $70,000 and the expenses of the sale were $5,000, you would be entitled to the balance of $50,000, computed as follows:

$$
\begin{array}{r}
\$70,000 \text{ sale price} \\
- \$15,000 \text{ loan balance} \\
- \$\ \underline{5,000 \text{ expenses}} \\
\$50,000 \text{ balance to you}
\end{array}
$$

I FOUND A BUYER FOR MY HOME PRIOR TO THE FORECLOSURE SALE WHO WILL PAY ME THE FULL $100,000 THAT MY HOME IS WORTH. CAN I SELL IT ON MY OWN AFTER THE FORECLOSURE ACTION HAS BEEN STARTED BUT BEFORE THE DATE OF THE FORECLOSURE SALE?

When a foreclosure action is pending, you will probably get a better price if you find your own buyer before
the date of the foreclosure sale. Legally, until a judgment
of foreclosure is entered, you are still the owner of your
home and you are entitled to sell it, just as if no foreclosure action is pending. So, if you can sell your home to
someone else before a judgment is entered, you have no
legal impediments to your sale. (You will have to pay off
your obligations with the proceeds of the sale, including
the outstanding mortgage that is the subject of the foreclosure action.)

If you can't schedule your sale to a private buyer until
after the judgment of foreclosure is entered, you may still
be able to go through with your private sale if you take
action prior to the scheduled date of the foreclosure sale.
You should contact the lender in advance of the foreclosure sale date and make arrangements to pay off the total
outstanding balance of the mortgage loan obligation by
closing on your private sale before the foreclosure date.

The bottom line is that the lender wants its money and
doesn't particularly care whether you pay it directly or get
the money from a bidder at a foreclosure sale. So, if you
send the lender all that is owed, the lender will see to it that
the foreclosure judgment is "vacated" (canceled) after you
send the check. Title to the property will return to you, and
you will have the right to sell your home to a private buyer.

IF I CAN'T BRING MY MORTGAGE PAYMENTS UP TO DATE AND I DON'T WANT TO LOSE MY HOME, IS THERE ANY-THING ELSE I CAN DO TO KEEP MY HOME?

If you're behind in your mortgage payments but don't
want to lose your home by foreclosure sale or private
sale, you may be entitled to file a bankruptcy proceeding
in federal bankruptcy court, which will stop a foreclosure

action against your home. There are also other consider-ations (discussed in the bankruptcy and creditors' rights section of this book) that may affect your decision whether or not to file a bankruptcy proceeding. However, it is an option to be considered by you and your attorney when facing an otherwise inevitable fore-closure action.

THE TOWN IS WIDENING THE STREET WHERE I LIVE AND THEY WANT TO TAKE A PORTION OF MY FRONT LAWN TO DO SO. WHAT ARE MY RIGHTS?

Your local or regional government may have the right to take a portion of your land, but they must pay you to do so. They may bring a lawsuit against you or negotiate a fair price with you. If your town wants to widen a street, which means cutting off a piece of your property, it will either start a lawsuit against you and all of your neigh-bors from whom it wishes to take property, or it may be entitled under local law to file a special condemnation map. Upon filing of the map, title will "vest" in (go into the name of) the governmental authority.

At the end of the lawsuit, if you have not already agreed in advance to give them a deed for the portion of land they want, they will get a court order declaring that they are the owner of the property and issue you a check for the appraised value of the land they are taking from you. Even if you disagree with the reasons for taking of your property and would prefer to retain your entire front lawn, the government has a superior right under the law to appropriate your land for public use.

I WANT TO OPEN MY OWN BUSINESS IN MY HOME. DO I NEED PERMISSION FROM THE LOCAL BUILDING DEPARTMENT?

Depending upon your local laws and the type of business you intend to operate, you may need a special permit to operate a business from your home, particularly if your business will have clients frequently visiting you (such as a doctor or dentist).

It's wise to check out these regulations prior to opening your business, or else you may run the risk of the building department shutting down your operation. In addition, if you live in a neighborhood with a homeowners' association, or in a condominium or cooperative apartment, business use of any part of your home may be prohibited in any form without permission of the applicable authority. Even if you want to operate a "cottage" industry from your home, such as sewing bridesmaids' and wedding dresses, the rules and regulations of your homeowners' association or condominium or co-op association might flatly prohibit any kind of business, whether or not you have clients or customers frequently visiting you. And if you choose to ignore these regulations, your neighbors may have the right to bring a lawsuit against you to terminate your home business operations.

I AM PLANNING TO RENT MY HOUSE OUT WHEN I GO ON AN OUT-OF-TOWN, THREE-YEAR WORK ASSIGNMENT. SHOULD I HAVE A WRITTEN LEASE?

Suppose you and your tenant had a written lease stating that the yearly rent for three years would be $6,000. After one year, your tenant moves out. You could sue the tenant for the second and third years' rent if you could not find a tenant to replace her. Without a written lease, the law presumes a month-to-month relationship, so the most you could sue the tenant for who moved out early would be one month's rent.

WHAT RIGHTS DO I GET (AS A LANDLORD) BY HAVING A WRITTEN LEASE?

Even if you plan to rent for a period shorter than a year, you may wish to have a written lease so that you may give yourself additional rights you might not otherwise be entitled to. A written lease could provide that in the event of default by the tenant, the tenant would pay your legal fees and costs to enforce the lease agreement. If there was no such written agreement, you would be hard-pressed to convince the court that the tenant had orally agreed to pay your attorney's fees.

WHAT TERMS SHOULD I INCLUDE IN MY WRITTEN LEASE AGREEMENT?

In addition to the essential terms of the lease agreement (duration of the lease, description of the property, amount of the rent, names of the parties), you may also want to include various other terms. You may wish to include the option to collect attorneys' fees in the event of default, as discussed above. You may also wish to provide that, as additional rent, the tenant will pay such things as the utility bills (electricity, water, sewer, etc.) and taxes on the property (or reimburse you for the taxes as they become due).

You may also want to include a cost-of-living adjustment in your rent computation of a long-term lease so that your rent income will keep pace with the cost of living. You could include a clause stating that the building will be used only as a residence and for no other purpose so that your tenant can't start a business, which may cause disharmony with your neighbors.

Tenants could be asked to maintain and repair the premises while they are living there, and told what items

they will be required to cover. For instance, you as landlord might require that the tenant keep an oil burner service contract in effect at all times so that if the heater
breaks down, you will not have to pay for repairs. Or you
might require that the tenant keep the lawn regularly cut
or the snow shoveled from the sidewalks as required.
Just as with other contracts, a well-thought-out lease
agreement can save you time and aggravation in the long
run.

I RETURNED FROM MY OUT-OF-TOWN ASSIGNMENT ONLY TO FIND THAT MY TENANTS HAD ABANDONED THE PREMISES I HAD RENTED TO THEM. IN ADDITION, MY TENANTS, UNBE-KNOWNST TO ME, USED MY HOUSE TO MANUFACTURE ILLEGAL DRUGS, CAUSING GROUND POLLUTION OF THE ADJOINING LAND. THE ENVIRONMENTAL PROTECTION AGENCY NOW INSISTS THAT I CLEAN UP THE MESS, WHICH WILL COST ABOUT $75,000. AM I RESPONSIBLE FOR THIS ENVIRONMENTAL CLEANUP?

As owner of the property, you are responsible for
cleaning up pollution originated from your property—
whether or not you, personally, had anything to do with
producing the pollution. Although there may be local or
federal funds you can apply for or subsidized loans available to assist you in this effort, the bottom line is that
you are liable for the cleanup costs.

It's unlikely that you'll ever be able to locate your former tenants to sue them for the damage they caused.
However, if the police arrest the tenants and also seize
cash or other assets, you may be able to collect your
cleanup costs from the seized assets.

Normally, in a rental situation, a security deposit is
retained by the landlord to guarantee that the premises
are returned in good condition, but, obviously, even

though the security deposit was forfeited by the tenants when they fled, in this situation it will not be nearly enough to compensate for the actual costs of the cleanup.

HOW CAN I PROTECT MYSELF TO MAKE SURE THAT I RENT TO A LAW-ABIDING AND FINANCIALLY RESPONSIBLE TENANT?

Unfortunately, there are no guarantees about the people you rent your home to, however respectable they may seem. You can take normal precautions, such as requesting a credit report on the prospective tenant, to see if he owes money to others and whether he pay his bills on time.

You should ask for and check references, particularly former landlords, to see whether the rent was paid on time, whether the tenant's behavior was respectable, and whether the premises were returned in good condition. You may find out that eviction proceedings were initiated every three months to keep the rent coming in from this tenant. Or you may find out that each time the tenant moved, he forfeited the security deposit due to the damage he caused to the rented space.

Verify employment status, or if the person is self-employed, request a financial statement from his accountant or a copy of his last two years' tax returns. If you find that his record of income is sporadic, you can expect that the payment of rent will be sporadic, too. If the proposed tenant refuses to disclose this information to you, you may not wish to rent to him, since he may have something to hide.

IF I AM RENTING A HOUSE OR APARTMENT, WHEN AM I ENTITLED TO GET MY SECURITY DEPOSIT BACK?

Unless your lease states that you get it back at another time, your security deposit will be returned after you move out and your landlord has inspected the premises to make sure that you didn't leave behind any damage to the property. If you left a big hole in the wall, your landlord will deduct the cost of covering the hole and repainting the wall before she returns your security deposit. If you left no damage and properly removed all of your personal belongings prior to your departure, you will get all of your security back.

If the landlord fails to return the security deposit, you should contact your lawyer, your state's attorney general's office, or take the case to small-claims court.

I RENTED AN APARTMENT SIX MONTHS AGO. NOW MY BOYFRIEND WANTS TO MOVE IN WITH ME. CAN HE?

If you have a lease, check it to see what it says about additional people moving in with you. You may be restricted to family members moving in with you, such as a spouse or children. Or you may be restricted to one unrelated person moving in with you. Your lease may prohibit anyone from living with you for more than two weeks at a time.

If you have no lease and a month-to-month arrangement with your landlord, your landlord can give you thirty days' notice to move out if she doesn't like the fact that your boyfriend moved in. So it's a good idea to check with your landlord before inviting your boyfriend to stay.

I HAVE A ROOMMATE WHO HASN'T PAID HER SHARE OF THE RENT FOR THREE MONTHS. AM I RESPONSIBLE?

If you both signed a lease agreeing to be responsible for the rent, your landlord can collect all the rent from one or both of you. If part of the rent is not paid and you refuse to pay your roommate's share, your landlord will be able to evict you both.

If you have no lease, unless the landlord agreed to collect rent separately from each of you (which is unlikely), he will be able to evict you both if the whole rent is not paid. If you want to keep your apartment and your roommate is not paying her fair share, do yourself a favor—get a new roommate.

SECTION 4

THE SMALL PRINT: SMART QUESTIONS TO ASK ABOUT CONTRACTS

Every day of our lives we deal with contracts. Whenever we make a purchase at the store, or have clothes dry-cleaned, or get a haircut, we are entering into contracts. Understanding our basic contract rights is important in conducting our daily affairs.

Problems with contracts occur when one person gets less than what she expected from the deal or one of the parties fails to live up to his side of the deal (by not delivering goods or not performing a service, or by not paying for the goods or services). Problems can be minimized if all parties to a contract fully understand what is expected of them and if each party fulfills his part of the bargain.

You may not need a lawyer when you enter into a contract to get your clothes cleaned or your hair cut. This section contains questions to ask your lawyer whenever you are about to enter into an agreement with another person or party and you run across areas of concern.

If there is anything in a contract you do not understand, *ask questions before you sign.* If you think the other party has not lived up to his or her end of the bargain, *ask questions* to be sure you are getting everything you've been promised.

WHAT CONSTITUTES A CONTRACT?

There are four necessary factors for a contract to be legally binding:

1. Both parties must have the legal capacity to make a contract (be of legal age and have the mental capacity to understand what the contract is about);
2. There must be an offer (a proposal to buy, sell, or do something);
3. There must be an acceptance of the offer (both parties have agreed with no strings attached); and
4. There must be consideration (something you give or do in return for something else, i.e., you give money in exchange for a service provided).

If any one of these four factors is missing, the contract is deemed to have never been completed, and it is not enforceable by either party. Let's say you agree to sell your stamp collection to a thirteen-year-old collector. Two weeks later he changes his mind. You could not enforce the contract against him because he is under the legal age to make legally binding contracts.

Several weeks later you have a general discussion with another prospective buyer, but never actually come up with a firm money offer. Neither party can enforce the contract at this point because there was no proposal to buy. If your buyer made an offer to purchase your stamp collection, but you decided to think about it for a few days, the buyer could not enforce the contract against you because you had not yet accepted her offer.

If you and the prospective stamp collection purchaser agree on all the terms of the contract, but she fails to show up with the agreed amount, you have no obligation to turn over the stamps until she delivers the purchase price to you.

WHEN MUST A CONTRACT BE IN WRITING?

In many cases, a handshake or an oral agreement is just as good as a written contract. But here are some instances when it must be in writing:

- *Contracts dealing with real estate, except for leases of less than a year.* If you made an oral agreement with someone to buy her house, the agreement would not be enforceable by either party until it's been put in writing.
- *Contracts for sale of goods costing more than $500.* If you say you'll sell your antique train collection to a buyer for $4,000, the oral contract isn't valid since it concerns goods in excess of $500. It must be in writing if either party wants to enforce it against the other.
- *Contracts that cannot be performed within one year from the date when the contract is made.* If you agree to ship televisions to a retailer each month for a period of two years, this agreement should be in writing, since it cannot be performed within one year.
- *Contracts that require services for the lifetime of either party.* An agreement to provide health care services

for the rest of someone's life should be in writing because it requires services to be performed for the lifetime of one of the parties.

- *Contracts in consideration of marriage, such as pre-marital and property settlement agreements.* Suppose you're getting married and you want to make some property settlement arrangements with your spouse-to-be (because you just inherited a great sum of money from your deceased parents). Such an agreement must be in writing in order to successfully enforce it later.

- *Promises to pay someone else's debts.* If you wish to personally guarantee your corporation's debts (in order to induce a supplier to send you goods), it must be in written form before the supplier can enforce the agreement against you.

IS THERE ANYTHING I CAN DO IF I THINK THE CONTRACT IS FRAUDULENT OR MISREPRESENTED WHAT I WAS GETTING?

You must take prompt action to cancel the contract or you may lose your right to do so. Suppose you buy a pedigree dog, and you find out it really isn't pedigree. If you then wait a year before you make a complaint, you may have given up your rights to get a full refund. You may get some money back, but your chances are slimmer the longer you wait.

However, if you never discovered the misrepresentation until after you've had the dog for a year, you may still have rights to cancel the contract even though time has elapsed, since you just now found out about the problem. As in any contract, you should carefully examine the products or services you are receiving as soon as possible to make sure you are getting what you paid for.

IF I ENTER INTO A VALID CONTRACT AND CHANGE MY MIND LATER, CAN I BACK OUT OF THE CONTRACT?

Unless there's a specific provision in the contract allowing you to cancel, you must follow through with the deal. Otherwise, the other party will have the right to recover damages from you for your refusal to honor the contract.

For instance, if you contract to sell your boat to someone but an hour later you get a better offer, you cannot call up the first buyer and cancel the contract unless the first buyer agrees to the cancellation. If you try to back out of the deal, the first buyer will have the right to start a lawsuit against you for damages he may have sustained because of your refusal to perform the contract. He may also be able to sue or to force you to go through with the deal.

AM I BOUND TO A CONTRACT I SIGNED EVEN IF I DIDN'T UNDERSTAND WHAT I WAS SIGNING?

Perhaps. Suppose you signed a contract to paint your house. What you didn't realize was that the painter could charge you interest if you didn't pay him in full within thirty days of completing the job. This contract will be enforceable even though you may not have understood all the technical terms in the contract.

However, suppose you thought you were signing a contract for a paint job, but it was actually a mortgage against your house in favor of the painter. You might be able to get out of this contract if you can prove you didn't understand what you were signing.

IF I GET A WRITTEN ESTIMATE FROM A CONTRACTOR, IS EITHER ONE OF US BOUND BY THAT DOLLAR FIGURE?

The estimate from the contractor represents an offer to do certain work for a specified price. If you ask the contractor to perform the work for that price, you are bound to pay the price if he completes the work.

If you think the estimate is too high, you should negotiate a better price before the contractor starts the job; if you don't, you will be bound by the original price. If you wait more than a "reasonable" amount of time (such as a year) before letting the contractor know you want the work done, he can increase his price; you can't hold him to his original estimate.

On the contractor's side, if after starting the job, he finds out that the work will take twice as long as anticipated because of a hidden defect in your house, the contractor can ask you to pay more to cover the cost of the additional work.

I WAS NEGOTIATING WITH SOMEONE TO BUY PART OF HER JEWELRY COLLECTION. WE AGREED ON EVERYTHING EXCEPT THE PRICE. I DECIDED TO BACK OUT OF THE DEAL, BUT SHE SAYS SHE WILL SUE ME IF I DON'T COMPLETE THE PURCHASE. WHAT ARE MY RIGHTS?

The parties must agree on all "material" terms of a contract before it is enforceable. In this case, the price was a material term of the contract; since there was no agreement on price, the contract is unenforceable.

However, if there was disagreement on another aspect of the deal (such as the exact place of delivery of the jewelry), it might not be considered a "material" term of the contract. The contract would be enforceable even though there was a portion of the deal on which you had not yet agreed.

Material terms can vary with each contract. If you initially agree to pay for the jewelry on Thursday, then call to say that you can't get the money until Saturday, this would not be considered to be a change in a material term of the contract. But if the seller had previously told you she was going out of the country on Friday and would not sell you the jewelry unless you agreed to pay her by Thursday, it would be considered a material term.

WHAT KIND OF DAMAGES CAN I GET IF SOMEONE REFUSES TO HONOR A CONTRACT WITH ME?

Depending upon the type of deal and the goods or services involved, you may be entitled to recover different types of damages. Let's say you have a valid contract to buy a microwave oven from your neighborhood merchant. He refuses to honor the contract. If you go out and find the same microwave oven in another store, but at a higher price, you may be entitled to recover the difference between the price in the contract and the price you actually had to pay.

Suppose you're a computer consultant and have a contract to work with a bank. You've turned down other opportunities in order to do this job. You may be entitled to recover your lost profits if the bank tries to cancel your contract.

Under some circumstances, you may be able to force the person to perform under his or her contract. Take a case like this: You contract to purchase some unique antique furniture from a reputable dealer. You show up with the purchase price, but he refuses to deliver the furniture. If you can prove that the furniture is truly unique and unavailable from other sources, a court may force the dealer to sell the furniture to you.

Courts will not generally try to force someone to perform if services instead of products are involved. A noted surgeon who had agreed to perform surgery on you, for example, but decided later against performing the surgery, will not generally be forced to perform such a personal service.

WHAT IF SOMEONE PERFORMS ON A CONTRACT, BUT THE GOODS OR SERVICES ARE DEFECTIVE? WHAT ARE MY RIGHTS?

If someone sells you defective goods, you may be entitled to such remedies as refund of the purchase price, exchange of the defective goods, or reimbursement of the cost to repair the goods.

Some states have laws concerning certain consumer goods, such as "lemon laws" for new cars, which spell out specific rights and remedies that cannot be altered by the new car dealer. For instance, if you bought a new car that needed a transmission replacement, a clutch replacement, and a steering box replacement within two weeks after you bought it, you may be able to force your car dealer to take back the "lemon" and sell you a brand new car.

Other retailers who are not so regulated may be able to change your rights under local law if their warranty restrictions meet certain requirements. Your local clothing store can prominently post a sign stating that all sale items are final and that there will be no exchanges or refunds once you've purchased the item. The warning "let the buyer beware" then comes into play, and if you later find out that there's a broken zipper in the pants you bought, you may be out of luck.

If someone performs defective services for you, you may be able to get your money back, or possibly the cost of having someone come in and properly complete the service.

IF UNEXPECTED CIRCUMSTANCES MAKE IT IMPOSSIBLE FOR ME TO HONOR MY END OF A CONTRACT, CAN THE OTHER PARTY FORCE ME TO PERFORM?

There are situations where a contract may be canceled if one party is unable to perform. For example, if you contract to sell your car to someone and the car is wrecked in a collision, the contract is deemed canceled and you must return the down payment to the buyer. Or, if you had contracted to have decorating services performed in your office, and the entire building was destroyed by fire before any work was started, the contract would be canceled because the object of the services was no longer in existence; your decorator could not successfully bring a lawsuit against you when you failed to pay her bill.

IF I HAVE A CLAIM AGAINST SOMEONE BASED UPON A CONTRACT BETWEEN US, HOW LONG DO I HAVE TO START A LAWSUIT AGAINST THEM?

You'll have to ask your attorney what the time period is. It will vary, depending upon the laws of your particular state, the type of contract, and the nature of the claim. It's important to consult an attorney as soon as possible after you think you have a claim so that your rights are not denied simply because you failed to start your lawsuit on time (see the section on lawsuits).

IF I SELL SOMEONE SOME GOODS AND THEY DO NOT PAY FOR THEM RIGHT AWAY, CAN I CHARGE THEM INTEREST ON THE UNPAID AMOUNT?

If the other party does not specifically agree to pay interest on past-due payments, you generally cannot charge interest on unpaid sums.

Case in point: You sell a grocery store a shipment of your homemade candy. The bill states that if it's not paid in thirty days, interest will be charged. You won't be able to enforce this unless the purchaser agrees in advance to pay interest if she's late in making payments. Even if you've been sending her such invoices for ten years, that does not, in itself, constitute an agreement to pay interest. But if the candy store owner signs a written contract with you stating that if she doesn't pay on time, she agrees to pay you interest, you can successfully collect interest from her if she fails to pay promptly.

I CAME HOME ONE DAY TO FIND THAT MY HOUSE HAD BEEN COMPLETELY REPAINTED. A PAINTER WAS STANDING IN THE DRIVEWAY WAITING FOR ME, AND DEMANDED THAT I PAY FOR THE PAINT JOB. IT TURNED OUT THAT THE PAINTER HAD PAINTED THE WRONG HOUSE ON THE WRONG STREET. DO I HAVE TO PAY FOR THE UNWANTED PAINT JOB?

If you had no knowledge that the painter was coming and didn't order a paint job, you won't have to pay. However, if you were home at the time the painters arrived, knew that you had not contracted for your house to be repainted, said nothing, and let them complete the job, you would be responsible for paying the fair value of the services rendered.

Similarly, if someone sends you goods through the mail that you didn't order, you don't have to pay for them. Nor do you necessarily have a duty to return the goods to the sender. Suppose you receive a book in the mail, addressed to you. The letter inside states that if you don't return the book in thirty days, you'll have to pay for it. Legally, the sender cannot force you to pay for the book.

If, however, the book was delivered to your address (with someone else's name on it) by mistake, you have a duty to call the company who sent it and tell them they made a mistake. If you don't, they may rightfully charge you for the book delivered to you, since you knew it was delivered to the wrong address and not really intended for you.

I'M ENTERING INTO A LONG-TERM LEASE WITH AN AUTO-MOBILE DEALERSHIP TO RENT THEM A COMPUTERIZED EMISSION-TESTING MACHINE, WHICH I MANUFACTURED AND DESIGNED. WHAT KINDS OF TERMS SHOULD WE PUT INTO THIS CONTRACT TO PROTECT MY RIGHTS AS OWNER OF THE MACHINE?

When leasing someone property that belongs to you, there are many important considerations. The lease should be in writing and contain all of the "material" terms, such as how much the payments are, where, when, and to whom the payments are to be made, and an exact description of the machine to be leased.

Your attorney may suggest that additional terms be added to the contract to protect your rights. For instance, the lease should contain a clause requiring the lessee to maintain fire, theft, and casualty loss insurance on the machine, with you named as loss payee. Then, if it's damaged, destroyed, or stolen, you'll be reimbursed for your loss.

The lease should also contain a clause requiring that the machine only be used at the location specified in the lease so that you'll always know where it is (in case you have to repossess it).

HOW CAN I PROTECT MYSELF AGAINST THE LESSEE DEFAULTING ON THE AGREEMENT?

The lease should clearly state what happens in event that the lessee doesn't live up to the lease agreement—by failing to make lease payments, failing to keep appro-

priate insurance coverage on the machine, or other failure. In the event of default in performance in one of the
terms of the lease, you'll want the right to declare the
lease in default, repossess the machine, and go after the
lessee for the balance of the lease payments.

Your attorney should also advise you of any governmental filings that you, as lessor, should make to establish ownership of the machine in your name even though
it is being used by the lessee (so your lessee can't try to
sell the machine to someone else).

I AM LOANING MY EMPLOYEE MONEY SO SHE CAN BUY A NEW CAR. HOW CAN I MAKE SURE MY RIGHTS ARE PROTECTED?

When you're loaning someone else money, you should
have a written loan agreement, just as a bank would, to
protect your rights as a lender. The exact terms of the
loan should be set forth, such as the full amount of the
loan, the amount of each loan payment, and when, where,
and to whom the payments are to be made. Your attorney
will also advise you whether the rate of interest you want
to charge is legal in your state.

What happens in case of default of the loan should be
clearly spelled out. You may want the loan to become
due in full if one payment is missed so that you can start
a lawsuit immediately for the entire amount of the loan
and not have to wait to sue for the entire amount. You
may want the right to repossess the car and sell it if your
employee stops making payments.

As you'll want to recover your expenses in the case of
default by your employee, you should provide that such
items as collection fees and attorney's fees are due you if
your employee defaults the agreement.

You'll want some provision in the loan agreement stating what happens if the employee wants to sell the car or

if the employee no longer works for you; you may want the loan to become due in full if either of these events happens. You might also want to file appropriate governmental forms to have your loan recorded as a lien against the car, so that the car can't be sold unless your loan is paid off first. Also, you should probably be named on your employee's car insurance policy as a loss payee in the event of theft or destruction of the car.

I AM ABOUT TO "SELL" MY SERVICES AS AN INDEPENDENT CONSULTANT TO AN OUTSIDE COMPANY. WHAT TERMS SHOULD I PUT IN THE AGREEMENT TO PROTECT MY RIGHTS?

There are many factors to be considered when entering into a contract to provide personal services. You should specify the exact job you're being asked to perform, and when you will perform it. Will you only work Monday through Friday from 9:00 A.M. to 5:00 P.M., with no overtime or weekends? Have you agreed to produce a certain result by a certain deadline? What happens if you miss the deadline (by two days or by two months)? How are you to be paid—by the hour or by the job? When will you be paid—daily, weekly, or at the end of the job? Will the company pay for certain benefits for you while you are on the job, such as the premiums on your health care insurance? Will you work holidays or will you receive extra pay for them? Will you perform the work at their office or at your office; if at their office, what services will they provide you with (photocopy machine, typing services, telephone services)? What happens if the company is supposed to give you something you need to complete your job but they give it to you four weeks late and you cannot complete the job on time? A carefully drafted agreement, in which you address all aspects of the work that may be important to you, may save you aggravation, time, and money. Even if you have drafted what you believe to be a great contract, you may want your attorney to review it to see whether you've covered all the important points.

YOU'RE THE BOSS: SMART QUESTIONS TO ASK ABOUT STARTING YOUR OWN BUSINESS

Nowadays, it seems as if starting your own business is part of the American dream. Every year, more and more people are leaving the corporate world and taking the plunge into life as an entrepreneur.

There are risks and there are rewards. There is no way to guarantee prosperity. But there are ways to minimize risk and to maximize potential success. One of the most important ways is to understand the legal aspects, and ramifications, of starting a business of your own.

Can you legally start a business in your home? Do you have the proper permits, licenses, zoning clearances? Who's taking responsibility for clients' injuries, complaints, or lawsuits? These are just a few of the issues involved. The questions in this section will give you a taste of what you need to know before you begin your great adventure; there may be other questions more relevant to your particular enterprise that you need to ask.

DO I NEED ANY SPECIAL LICENSES, PERMISSION, OR OTHER GOVERNMENTAL APPROVAL TO OPEN AND MAINTAIN MY BUSINESS (E.G., PROFESSIONAL LICENSE, BUILDING DEPARTMENT SPECIAL-USE PERMIT, LIQUOR LICENSE, ETC.)?

There are many variables involved in answering this question—depending on where you live, and what kind of business you want to open. Each state has different laws as to what special licenses or permits are required by your business.

Let's start with an example involving medicine. Before you practice medicine, you must receive a professional license from your state to do so. If you then want to open a medical office, you'll have to consult your local building department rules and regulations to determine where you can do that. If your proposed office is in a residential area, you may need special permission to use a part of your house for that purpose. If you want to convert an abandoned warehouse in an industrial section of town into a medical office, you may need to apply to have the zoning for that particular piece of property changed.

If, instead, you want to open a restaurant in which you intend to serve alcoholic beverages, you'll have to get a liquor license from your state. You'll probably need a permit from the local department of health before you can legally serve food to others. And you may also need a public assembly permit before your first customer can legally walk through the door.

Before you open any business you should be sure that you have obtained all of your required licenses or permits to avoid unnecessary delays.

WHAT LEGAL FORM SHOULD MY BUSINESS TAKE—SOLE PROPRIETORSHIP, PARTNERSHIP, OR CORPORATION?

Normally, a corporation offers limited personal liability for the owners of a business; therefore new business operators should consider this form of ownership. It would be to your advantage to form a corporation so that if someone was hurt while on your premises, any recovery by the injured person would be limited to the assets of the corporation, and your personal assets could not be claimed.

On the other hand, in a sole proprietorship or a partnership, an injured person could collect a judgment from your personal assets, including your personal residence, bank accounts, stocks, and other assets that you had worked so hard to accumulate.

However, if you fall within a certain group of "professional" persons, such as doctors, lawyers, dentists, and architects, you may not be able to escape personal liability for the work you produce. The laws of your state may prohibit you from hiding behind the corporate shield if someone is damaged or injured by you in the course of performance of your profession. (The state exacts this penalty from the professional in exchange for his or her professional license, which is an exclusive right to work in that particular field.)

IF I FORM A CORPORATION, AM I PROTECTED FROM ALL PERSONAL LIABILITY?

Don't think that by forming a corporation you can do whatever you want and escape all accountability. Even if you form a corporation, you may still be personally responsible for certain business debts, including payroll-related taxes, sales tax, and other matters that your business failed to pay.

Suppose you deducted federal and state income taxes from your employees' paychecks but failed to turn over the money to the proper taxing authority. As an officer of the corporation, you (and any other officers) can be held personally liable for paying these taxes. Similarly, if your store collected sales tax on items you sold, but your bookkeeper used the money to take a trip to South America (where she is today), you, as an officer of the corporation, can be held personally responsible for this obligation.

Also, certain acts by officers, shareholders, or directors of a corporation may subject them to personal liability even if done under the guise of working for the corporation. If your corporation intentionally defrauded your customers by misrepresenting the effectiveness of your new hair-loss-prevention product, you (as a principal of the corporation who actively participated in the perpetration of the fraud) may be held personally liable for the consequences. This is because you are considered to have acted beyond the scope of the business of your corporation when committing a fraud. You should review these items of potential personal liability with your attorney before you start your business.

IF I FORM A CORPORATION, WON'T MY CORPORATION HAVE TO PAY ADDITIONAL TAXES?

This depends on the type of corporation formed. A corporation may receive similar income tax treatment to a sole proprietorship or a partnership and not be subject to "double taxation" (i.e., taxing of income to both the corporation and then to the shareholder as he or she receives it in salary). The corporation may have to file a separate income tax return each year and/or issue income statements of monies paid to its shareholders. So income tax considerations may not constitute a disadvantage to a new business operator.

A corporation will also be subject to "franchise" taxes, imposed by individual states for the privilege of doing business in that state, and a franchise tax return must be filed each year. If the advantage of having limited liability outweighs the disadvantage of having to pay corporation franchise taxes, it is worth the extra money to do business in the form of a corporation. Your applicable business and tax laws will assist you and your lawyer in deciding what form of business yours should take.

I AM BUYING AN EXISTING BUSINESS FROM SOMEONE ELSE. WHAT FACTORS SHOULD I CONSIDER?

Buying an existing business can be more complicated than starting up your own. There are a number of items to be considered before you make any decision to buy:

1. For tax purposes, you'll want to consider whether you should purchase the business assets (the physical plant, machinery, etc.) or buy the corporation's stock (if any). From a buyer's point of view, an acquisition of the business assets will provide more favorable tax consequences. However, a seller will receive better tax treatment if a sale of the stock of the corporation is made. This is often a confusing issue for lawyers as well as their clients, so ask as many questions as you need to make sure you understand your options.

2. Another consideration is how to prevent the former owner from opening up his own business in competition with your new business after he or she sells it to you. If you negotiate a promise with the seller not to compete with your new business for a cer-

tain period of time after you take over (say five years) or within a certain geographical area (say, one hundred miles), you can protect yourself against such competition.

3. You may wish to encourage certain key employees to stay with the company when you take over. Therefore, you may wish to get employment contracts with these people so that you will know that they will be available to assist you in the transition between the old owner and your new business.

4. You should verify, through governmental filing offices, whether there are any judgments or liens against the existing business you are taking over, either against the company in general or against the specific assets of the business (such as machinery or vehicles). On any bank liabilities you are taking over, you will want statements from the lenders as to how much is owing and the exact payback terms.

5. You and/or your accountant should verify the receivables, as well as the inventory (including client lists) you are paying for as part of the deal.

6. You may want to use the same business name as the former owner to ease transition into your new business; you should arrange that this is part of the deal.

You must weigh the advantages of taking over a business that is "up and running" with the disadvantages of worrying about the above items when choosing whether to acquire an existing business or whether to start something on your own.

SHOULD I GET INVOLVED IN A BUSINESS FRANCHISE ARRANGEMENT?

If you like an already existing structure, but don't want the hassles of taking over someone else's business, a franchise may be the answer for you. If you purchase a franchise, the "mother" company will provide a setup and marketing scheme for you, and assist you in opening a new business using their techniques, name, and reputation.

In a women's clothing franchise, for example, the mother company may help you select the site, plan advertising campaigns, order your merchandise, and select and train your employees. (If you opened a business independently, you'd be doing all of these things on your own.) They may set you up in a specific geographic location, or assign you a specific territory, and guarantee that they will not issue any other franchises to someone else in your location or territory without your written permission. On the other hand, you'll be compelled to operate your business up to the standards set by the parent company, and you may not like to be limited in your business procedures. You may be limited to purchasing your inventory from a specified vendor in your area, instead of from another vendor who may have a better price or is a friend of yours.

You'll have to decide whether the instant structure afforded by a franchise arrangement is worth the limitations imposed.

WHAT KINDS OF BUSINESS INSURANCE SHOULD I PURCHASE?

You may be required by law or may wish to consider various types of insurance, including the following:

1. Workers' compensation insurance: This protects workers who are injured on the job in the course of their employment. If an employee of your office slips and falls and fractures his skull on the corner

of a desk, he would be covered by workers' compensation insurance and the costs of his hospitalization and doctors' bills would be payable from this source of insurance. As an employer, you may be required by law to maintain this type of insurance.

2. Disability insurance: This benefits workers who become ill or injured and are unable to work. Let's say that the employee in the above example was out of work for twelve weeks as a result of his injury. During his period of incapacity, he may be entitled to receive disability insurance payments from the disability insurance carrier. This type of insurance may be required by local or state law.

3. Liability insurance: This protects you against fire, theft, catastrophe, or injury of a nonemployee. If a customer of yours (instead of a worker) had the same fractured skull injury, she would be covered under your liability insurance policy, and the costs of her hospitalization and doctors' bills would be paid from this source. Although not mandatory, this type of insurance may be recommended by your advisers since you'll probably want to protect your business from fire or other loss. In order to obtain a local business license (such as a contractor's license), you may be required to carry liability insurance coverage.

4. Business interruption insurance: This protects your income if your business should be interrupted by catastrophe such as fire, flood, or earthquake. If your office were destroyed, business interruption insurance would pay for a limited amount of your monthly obligations (such as rent, equipment rental, and services) while you were unable to generate your own income. If you have high monthly overhead expenses or business debt (for example,

lines of credit to pay for merchandise), you may wish to consider this type of insurance so that in the event of a catastrophe, you'll be able to meet your monthly obligations.

5. Life insurance: This will provide a cash payment to a designated beneficiary upon death. If you have partners in your business, you may want to purchase life insurance on each other's lives so if one of you dies, the others can have ready cash to purchase the deceased's interest in the business from the heirs. If you have business debts for which you are personally responsible, you may wish to purchase life insurance on your own life so your estate is not depleted by claims of your business creditors.

AS AN EMPLOYER OF MYSELF AND OTHERS, WHAT PAYROLL-RELATED TAXES MUST I PAY?

Federal, state, and local laws require that certain payroll-related taxes, such as income tax, social security tax, and disability tax, be deducted from an employee's paycheck and paid to the appropriate governmental authority. When you pay your employees each week (two weeks, etc.) you have the responsibility of deducting all applicable governmental taxes from your employees' paychecks before you issue a check to them for the balance.

These laws also require an employer to contribute toward these taxes on behalf of the employee. You are required by law to contribute a certain percentage of your employees' gross pay for social security, federal income taxes, and state income tax (if any). Periodic payments to the government must be made by the employer for these taxes. You should be sure you ask your attorney and/or accountant to help you set up a collection and payment system for these payroll-related taxes.

CAN I HIRE AND FIRE MY EMPLOYEES AT WILL?

Unless you discriminate based upon a category prohibited by law, such as race, creed, color, sex, religion, national origin, etc., you can generally hire and fire your employees for any reason or no reason at all. You can refuse to hire someone, otherwise qualified, if she is a smoker and you do not like smoking.

If you do fire an employee for no reason at all, however, be prepared for a lawsuit. She may file a claim stating she was fired because you discriminated against her based upon one of the prohibited categories.

The rules become very different if your employees are unionized and you have agreed in writing to certain hiring and firing practices. You probably won't be able to fire a union employee unless you have good cause and you have held a hearing, attended by union representatives, at which you proved the reasons for the dismissal. If a unionized employee has attained tenure, he may have additional rights, such as the right not to be fired unless he commits a crime or some other act that seriously jeopardizes the business of the employer.

You should find out what you can and cannot do so that an unhappy employee doesn't surprise you with a lawsuit after he or she is fired by you. Firing an employee may also affect how much unemployment insurance you end up paying. Ask your attorney to recommend proper hiring and firing practices to you, based upon your local law and your contractual obligations. You can also check with the federal Equal Employment Opportunity Commission's public information service by calling 1-800-872-3362.

HOW CAN I PROTECT MYSELF AGAINST LAWSUITS BY FORMER EMPLOYEES AFTER I FIRE THEM?

First of all, try not to fire employees unless you have a good reason. Keep accurate records of the behavior of the employee that caused him to be fired.

If you fired an employee because of dishonesty, gather the information necessary to show that he was stealing from you, such as dates of each incident and what was stolen. If another employee witnessed the event, ask her to write down notes on what she saw so she can refer to them if she later has to testify in court.

If you fired an employee for incompetence, make a list of the specific tasks that your employee could not or would not perform, a list of the dates on which you discussed these inadequacies with your employee (you probably gave him at least one chance to improve his behavior before firing him), and what improvement, if any, occurred after your meetings. Armed with this information, you will be in a good position to defend a lawsuit if one is brought against you.

SHOULD I HAVE EMPLOYEE AGREEMENT LETTERS TO PREVENT THEM FROM SUING ME LATER IF THEY ARE FIRED?

Even if your employee signed an agreement, unless he was represented by his own attorney before he signed the agreement, he can claim he didn't understand the agreement or was forced to sign it to get the job, and therefore you took unfair advantage of him. So it may not make sense to have your employees sign agreements, since they may be declared unenforceable in court for the above reasons.

I HAVE LURED A VALUABLE PERSON FROM ANOTHER COMPANY TO COME AND WORK FOR ME. SHE INSISTED THAT WE HAVE A WRITTEN EMPLOYMENT AGREEMENT. WHAT TERMS SHOULD I AGREE TO?

There are many important terms that should be considered when entering into an employment contract, including job description, rate of pay, benefits, and under what terms employment can be terminated. A job description could include items such as the willingness to travel up to two weeks out of every month. You may wish to determine a level of pay for the first year and then limit increases to cost-of-living increases plus a bonus to be paid or not paid each year at your discretion (or related to increases in her sales for your company). You may wish to limit benefits to medical benefits for her, but not for her family. You may also want to compel her to give you six weeks' notice if she intends to leave your employ.

Even though she may want the employment agreement for her own benefit, you can negotiate some clauses in your favor, such as those suggested above. A properly drafted employment agreement can protect both the employer and the employee and serve as the basis for a good working relationship.

A NON-ENGLISH-SPEAKING PERSON CAME TO MY MANUFACTURING FACTORY AND APPLIED FOR EMPLOYMENT. I THINK SHE MAY BE AN ILLEGAL ALIEN. CAN I REFUSE TO HIRE HER UNLESS SHE PROVES SHE IS LEGALLY ENTITLED TO WORK IN THIS COUNTRY?

You cannot refuse to hire her merely because you suspect she is an illegal alien, since it's unlawful to discriminate on the basis of national origin or citizenship status. However, it is unlawful to knowingly hire someone who is an illegal alien. Under current law, all employers must seek written proof that employees they hire are legally entitled to work in this country.

In the above example, you as the employer must ask for written proof, such as a U.S. passport, U.S. citizenship or naturalization papers, or unexpired work visa, which show that your prospective employee is legally entitled to work. If she fails to produce such proof, you may legally refuse to hire her. Significant civil and criminal penalties will result from failing to comply with immigration laws, so it's important that you become acquainted with the guidelines employers must follow.

ONE OF MY EMPLOYEES COMPLAINED THAT HIS SUPERVISOR IS SUBJECTING HIM TO ACTS OF SEXUAL HARASSMENT ON THE JOB. WHAT ARE MY LIABILITIES AS EMPLOYER?

You have a duty to investigate accusations of sexual harassment on the job to make sure that none of your employees is violating any civil rights laws, including laws prohibiting sexual discrimination in the form of sexual harassment. If you ignore these reports and hope that the behavior will go away on its own, you may soon be faced with a discrimination complaint initiated by a federal or local agency accusing not only the supervisor but you, as the employer, of unlawful discrimination. Violations of civil rights laws carry civil and possibly criminal penalties, so you and your attorney should establish a procedure by which all such complaints are investigated and remedied, if necessary.

MY NEW BUSINESS HAS BECOME TREMENDOUSLY SUCCESSFUL, AND I THINK THAT IF I HAD SOME MORE MONEY TO INVEST IN NEW MANUFACTURING EQUIPMENT, I COULD QUADRUPLE THE BUSINESS I NOW HAVE. ONE OF MY BUSINESS ADVISERS SUGGESTED THAT I "GO PUBLIC" TO RAISE THE NECESSARY CASH. IS THAT A GOOD IDEA?

If you have a business that you think could benefit from additional outside capital, you may wish to consider "going public." Going public is a process by which small, operator-owned "private" companies issue additional shares of stock in their corporation to sell to outside investors, who contribute money into the business in exchange for the stock.

The advantages of going public include getting perhaps an otherwise unavailable influx of money from outside investors to pursue your business goals. However, there are other factors, which may present possible disadvantages. The expenses of going public can be great, and can exceed half a millon dollars or more for underwriters' fees, printing costs, accounting fees, and legal fees.

Also, once your corporation goes public, you are subject to the scrutiny of outside investors, who have nothing to do with the day-to-day running of your business, but who now have input at shareholders' meetings in electing the officers and directors of your corporation. You'll also now be obliged to file periodic reports with the federal Securities and Exchange Commission; your state's securities laws may also require you to making filings.

If you decide to become a private company again, you'll have to purchase your stock back from the outside investors (and they will want to see a profit from their investment).

After considering the pros and cons of going public, you and your advisers may decide that your cash requirements would be better met by getting a large bank loan to keep your ownership and control of the business.

MY BUSINESS PARTNER TOLD ME SHE WANTS TO BREAK UP. WHAT CAN I DO TO MAKE SURE MY RIGHTS ARE PROTECTED?

The first thing to do is find out whether your partner wants to break up and start a competing business, or whether she simply wants to retire and pursue other (business or nonbusiness) interests.

A retiring partner may be relatively easy to deal with since you may already have an agreement with your partner as to how you will buy each other out in the event someone wants to leave the business. An unhappy partner who wants to break off and start her own business may also be covered by a prior business agreement, which will spell out what will happen if one partner wants to leave.

But what if you have no agreement? If there is no prior agreement, some of the same potential problems arise as when you're buying an existing business from someone else. Who can use the existing business name (telephone number, address, trade name)? Will the breaking-off partner be competing for the same customers or clients? If one partner keeps the existing business, what about the existing liabilities (known and unknown) at the time of breakup? A simple "good-bye" may not be enough; you and your attorney should negotiate a dissolution agreement that covers all of your business concerns.

WHAT KINDS OF AGREEMENTS SHOULD I HAVE WITH MY BUSINESS PARTNERS REGARDING WHAT HAPPENS WHEN ONE OF US DIES?

A typical agreement contains limitations as to what partners can do with their business interests both before and after death. The agreement may provide that before your partner can sell her business interest to others, or upon her death, you must have the right of first refusal to buy out her share of the business. The agreement may further provide a price (that is regularly updated) that represents the value of the business for the purposes of the buyout. In this way, if a partner wants to retire, or dies, there is a set procedure and price that will make negotiation unnecessary in transferring the business over to the other partner.

A written business agreement can make for an easy transition in times of change, such as retirement or death of a partner.

Unless such an agreement is in writing, you're taking a chance that you might end up being partners with the deceased's spouse or children.

I'M A COMPUTER CONSULTANT, AND I HAVE DEVELOPED SOME SOPHISTICATED TRAINING MANUALS I USE TO TEACH OTHERS TO OPERATE THEIR COMPUTERS. HOW CAN I PROTECT OTHERS FROM COPYING MY MANUALS AND USING THEM?

If you properly copyright your computer training manuals, you'll be protected against unauthorized use of your written work. Before you let anyone use your training manuals, you and/or your attorney can file for copyright protection, which is governed by federal laws.

Although a copyright is obtained as soon as work is set down in written form, you should apply for federal copyright protection to get additional benefits, such as the ability to sue for infringement damages and to recover attorney's fees against someone who uses your work without permission. If you plan to market your training techniques, the smart thing to do would be to apply for copyright protection first so that your work will be protected from copying and use by others.

MY PARTNERS AND I HAVE PERFECTED A NEW TECHNIQUE FOR APPLYING CHROME TO AUTOMOBILE PARTS THAT WILL MAKE THEM VIRTUALLY RUST-PROOF. HOW CAN I PROTECT THIS PROCESS FROM UNAUTHORIZED COPYING AND USE BY OTHERS?

If you properly register your process with the United States Patent Office, no one will be able to use your new process without your permission. (If you think your process may be marketable internationally, you may wish to take the necessary steps to have it registered on an international basis.) Usually, the guidance of a patent attorney (often someone with a scientific or engineering background) is necessary to assist you in processing your patent applications. Part of the application process is that you prove that your process is unique and that no one else has previously applied for a patent for the same process.

If your process leaks out to the public before you can secure the patent registration, a user can claim it was in the "public domain" (that is, in the hands of the public), and therefore should not be afforded patent protection as a new process (or they may try to beat you to the punch by registering it before you do). So you should try to keep your process as "secret" as possible.

If you develop a new product, such as a simplified, labor-saving tool, you should get patent protection before you start using it so that anyone who wants to manufacture and sell your new tool will have to contact you first and obtain your permission (for a fee, of course!).

I HAVE DEVELOPED A CATCHY NAME FOR MY NEW LINE OF LONG-WEARING LIPSTICKS. HOW CAN I PROTECT THE NAME FROM BEING USED BY OTHERS?

If you have a name you have created for a new product or service, you can file to have the name registered as a trademark. Trademark law is federally controlled, so that if your trademark is properly registered, no one in the United States can use the name without your permission. (Again, you may wish to consider international registration if you think the name has international flair.)

In the past, part of the trademark application process was to show that you had publicly used the name for your product or service so that it had become a valuable business commodity in need of protection from unauthorized use by others. Now, you can apply for trademark registration prior to the sale of your product or service. Your goal should be to obtain trademark registration before the name becomes widely used by others to describe the same product or service (like Kleenex or Xerox).

CROSSED PURPOSES: SMART QUESTIONS TO ASK ABOUT LAWSUITS

I had a neighbor once who liked to tell tall tales. And sometimes he would make promises he couldn't keep. If you should happen to catch him in a lie or confront him about an unfulfilled commitment, his standard reply was, "So, sue me!"

His transgressions were never of a serious nature, and no one ever took him up on his dare. You may one day find yourself in a situation, however, where someone has broken a significant promise to you. Perhaps they didn't live up to a contract. Perhaps they owe you money, goods, or services. You may have no other recourse than to sue.

On the other hand, you may be the one who is being sued. What if you were involved in an auto accident, and the other driver thinks it's your fault? What if someone was injured on your property? What if you failed to make proper restitution to a creditor?

Whether you're suing or being sued, you must be sure that you understand your legal rights and responsibilities. By asking smart questions, you may be able to avoid a lawsuit, and find alternate means of settling your dispute. Or you may be able to collect more damages than you originally suspected.

Don't let a lawyer, yours or anyone else's, intimidate you. If you there's anything you don't understand, keep asking until you're satisfied with the answer.

I WANT TO SUE MY NEXT-DOOR NEIGHBOR FOR THE DAM-AGE CAUSED WHEN A TREE HE WAS CHOPPING DOWN IN HIS YARD LANDED ON MY GARAGE ROOF. HOW DO I START A LAWSUIT AGAINST HIM?

First, check your insurance to see if this type of damage is covered under your policy.

If you do sue, you must first properly "serve" him with legal papers so that he has notice of the claim you're making against him and an opportunity to be heard in connection with your claim.

In some states, such as New Jersey, the sheriff must serve the papers. In other states, you can have a process server (someone who delivers legal papers for a living) personally deliver the proper papers to him at his home or at his place of business. If the process server can't find him, your state law will provide alternative methods of how you can serve him.

The process server may be able to leave the legal papers with your neighbor's wife and then mail a copy to that home address. Or, if the process server makes several trips to his home, but no one is ever home, the process server may be able to "nail and mail" the papers by affixing a copy to the door of the home and then mailing another copy to that address.

If your neighbor skips town to avoid service upon him, you may still be able to get a court order providing for an alternative method of service (such as publishing the notice in an area newspaper) if you have exhausted all reasonable efforts to locate his whereabouts.

WHAT KIND OF LEGAL PAPERS MUST BE SERVED ON THE PERSON AGAINST WHOM I HAVE THE CLAIM?

Depending upon the type of claim you have, the papers you serve may have different names, such as summons and complaint, notice of petition and petition, or notice of claim and claim. However, they all have basically the same purpose: to let your adversary know the nature of your claim. If you're suing for a divorce, for example, you must state in your complaint the reasons why you are seeking a divorce (no-fault, infidelity, abandonment, cruelty, etc.), and what legal remedy you're looking for (such as a court order of divorce, alimony, and child support).

If you ask for nothing, that's what you'll get—so you and your attorney should try to make sure that you include all of your demands in the initial papers. Suppose you hired a landscaper to redo your front lawn. Not only did he fail to finish installing the sod, he also left a large hole in the ground—into which you fell one dark night and broke your ankle. When you bring a suit against your landscaper, you'll have to mention both the breach of contract (for failing to finish the job) and the negligence (for the leaving the hole you fell into) in order to have both issues addressed. You may be entitled to amend your papers if you forget something, but if you wait too long, your time limits may expire and you may lose the right to pursue the claim.

CAN I SUE SOMEONE FOR ANY REASON AT ALL, OR ARE THERE LEGAL LIMITATIONS?

In order to have a valid claim against someone, you generally must have:

- monetary damages (such as loss of profits); or
- a legal status you want changed or modified (such as changing your marital status by getting a divorce); or
- a behavior of another you want started or stopped (such as getting a contractor to stop demolition of an historic building).

Suppose your florist breached a contract to deliver flowers to your daughter's wedding, but you were able to get another florist to come in at the last minute with flowers just as lovely and at a better price. Even though your feelings were hurt and you were extremely upset, you would have no claim since you had no monetary damages (hurt feelings are generally not compensable under the law). On the other hand, if the substitute florist could not get exactly the flowers you wanted and charged you a 30 percent higher price because of overtime paid to employees to arrange the flowers at the last minute, you would have a valid claim against the first florist for the extra money you had to spend. In addition to your having a valid type of claim, the facts of your particular situation must support such a claim under the law.

HOW DO I KNOW IF THE FACTS OF MY PARTICULAR SITUATION SUPPORT A VALID CLAIM UNDER THE LAW?

The only way you can know is by asking your lawyer questions. You and your attorney will meet and discuss whether the facts of your particular case support a valid claim under the law. You can't sue someone just because you're angry, upset, or want to get even. If the only reason you want a divorce is that your spouse likes to eat crackers in bed, there may not be sufficient basis under your local law to permit a divorce. Your state's laws may limit the grounds to sue for a divorce to specific categories, such as abandonment, cruel or unusual treatment, adultery, or imprisonment.

Suppose you agree to buy someone's house, but the agreement was never put in writing. You don't have sufficient grounds to compel that person to sell, since a contract for the sale of real property must be in writing.

Let's take the florist in the previous question. What if he had been waiting for you to furnish the exact date for your daughter's wedding? He called you several times, but you never got back to him. In this scenario, you failed to perform a portion of your side of the contract, therefore the facts of your case do not support a valid claim.

WHAT KIND OF PROOF MUST I HAVE TO PROVE MY CLAIM IN A LAWSUIT?

You may present written proof or oral testimony of yourself or others to prove your claim.

If you present written proof, you must bring original documents to court (not photocopies), unless you can prove that the original documents were lost. So, if your claim is based upon a written contract, you must bring your original contract to court to present in evidence.

If you intend to present oral testimony, the person testifying must appear in person and cannot present testimony recorded on videotape or tape recorder. (This is so your adversary will have the right to cross-examine the witness and ask her questions to clarify or disprove her testimony.) So if you intend to call a passenger in your car as a witness in your car accident lawsuit, make sure she will be available to testify when your case goes to trial.

I THINK I HAVE A VALID CLAIM, BUT MY ATTORNEY SAYS I HAVE NO "STANDING" TO SUE. WHAT DOES THAT MEAN?

Your thirty-five-year-old son's wife beats him on a regular basis. You, as his mother, want to start a lawsuit against your belligerent daughter-in-law to force her to be divorced from your son. You would not be able to do this; your son would be the only person who would have standing to sue for a divorce against his wife. Proper "standing" to sue means that you are the appropriate party to start the lawsuit.

If, however, your son was mentally or physically incapable of bringing a lawsuit himself (if he had suffered a stroke, for example, and could not move or speak), you could petition the court to be appointed as his legal representative so that you could properly start a lawsuit on his behalf.

THERE ARE SEVERAL DIFFERENT COURTS IN MY AREA. HOW DO I KNOW WHICH ONE TO START MY LAWSUIT IN?

In your city or county, there may be a separate court for settling family matters, another one for criminal justice, and a third just for civil suits. There may be a special court in your area that handles only deceased person's affairs, and no other court may have the legal authority to hear cases concerning wills and estates. If you want to get a court order to prevent your ex-spouse from breaking into your house in the middle of the night to torment you, you may have to bring your petition in a court specially set up to handle family matters.

Sometimes, money makes the difference in where your case is heard. Different levels of courts are set up according to the amount of money being sought in civil cases. For instance, if your claim is $6,000 or less, you may have to use a local court; for a claim of between $6,000 and $10,000, you may use a county court; and for a claim in excess of $10,000, you may have to use the state court.

Sometimes, the type of remedy you're seeking determines the court you must use. If you're seeking low money damages, but you're also asking the court to stop the building of a shopping center next to your home, you may have to go to a state court. That may be the only court with the power to issue an order to stop the building of the shopping center.

After reviewing the nature of your claim and the type of relief you're looking for, you and your attorney will choose the appropriate court that has the power to hear your case and grant you the remedy you are seeking.

IF I GO TO COURT, WILL MY CASE BE HEARD BY A JUDGE, A JURY, OR BY SOMEONE ELSE?

This can depend on which court you're in, or whether you or your adversary wants to demand a trial by jury. Your case may be heard by a judge alone, or by a judge and jury. In some areas, if you have a small claim for money damages only, an arbitrator (appointed by the court) instead of a judge will be assigned to hear your case (although you may later have the right to request a trial before a judge if you don't like the arbitrator's decision).

IS IT TO MY ADVANTAGE TO HAVE MY CASE HEARD BEFORE A JUDGE?

In many courts, your case will be heard before a judge unless you or your adversary demands a jury trial in writing. This could be to your advantage. For instance, if you have a complex patent-infringement case involving complicated computer-related testimony, you may prefer that a well-educated judge decide your case because you feel there is a greater chance that someone with a higher level of education will understand the nature of your claim and be able to comprehend expert testimony. However, even if you and your attorney strategically decide that you would prefer presenting your case to a judge for a decision, your adversary may foil you by requesting a trial by jury, which may favor your adversary's case. Similarly, there may be times when you would prefer having a trial by jury, such as if you, as a consumer, are suing a multinational corporation for damage to you when a product they manufactured blew up in your face. Once you demand a trial by jury, unless you change your mind, your adversary cannot force you to go before a judge instead.

I HAVE HEARD THAT OUT-OF-COURT, PRIVATELY HANDLED ARBITRATION IS A BETTER METHOD OF RESOLVING DISPUTES. IS PRIVATE ARBITRATION AN OPTION I SHOULD CONSIDER?

If you and your adversary both agree (either in a contract that you are seeking to enforce or later, after there has been a dispute), you can choose to go to arbitration outside the court system. An organization, such as the American Arbitration Association, can assist you and your adversary in agreeing upon a mutually acceptable arbitrator to hear your case.

An advantage to private arbitration is that you may be able to request someone who is not a lawyer (most court-appointed arbitrators are lawyers), but rather an expert in the field that is the subject of your dispute. For instance, if you have a dispute about a defective piece of manufacturing equipment, you may be able to get an engineer to act as an arbitrator. Another advantage is that if your local courts are backlogged with trials, your case may be able to be heard within a matter of months instead of your waiting a longer period of time.

You may not be able to use an arbitrator under all circumstances. For instance, if you are seeking a divorce, an arbitrator will not have the power to issue a court order granting a divorce. Also, a private arbitrator may not have the power to subpoena reluctant witnesses to appear at the arbitration hearing, since only a judge has the power to compel a third party to testify.

HOW LONG DO I HAVE TO SUE?

Twenty years ago you were hit by a car. Now your back is aching and you decide it's a direct result of that unfortunate event. Can you sue after all this time? Probably not. Every case is subject to a statute of limitations (a time limit on when you can file a lawsuit). The time you have depends on the kind of case and varies from state to state.

In New York State, for instance, you may have three years to begin your lawsuit against the driver of a car that hit yours. On the other hand, if you want to sue to compel your neighbor to stop using a portion of your backyard as his rock garden, you may have ten years within which to start the lawsuit. If you have a contract to buy an automobile and it has been breached by the other party, you may have six years to commence the court action. If a doctor who was supposed to remove your gallbladder removed your appendix instead, causing you injury, you may have two and a half years to sue. If you were induced by fraud to enter into a bad business deal, you may have only two years after you discovered the fraud to start your lawsuit. If someone who was angry came to your home and hit you over the head with a baseball bat, you may have only one year within which to commence your court action against the person who battered you. If you were hurt by reason of the act of a public employee in the course of his employment (for instance, you were in an motorcycle accident with a municipal garbage truck whose driver ran a red light), you may have to file a notice of claim with the governmental office within ninety days of the claim, or you will forfeit all of your rights.

If you think you have a claim against someone, find out right away from your attorney how long you have to sue. Otherwise you may later be surprised to find out that your otherwise valid claim has been forfeited by you because you did not start your lawsuit in time.

HOW LONG WILL IT TAKE BEFORE MY LAWSUIT IS CONCLUDED?

Your matter could be settled in a few days. Or you could be old and gray by the time you get to trial, depending upon the tactics your adversary tries to use and the court in which you're suing.

If your adversary wants to fight your lawsuit, many things can happen. Your adversary can have his attorney do such (legal) things as request depositions and documents, file papers to get all or a part of your case dismissed, or seek postponements of any of the above. You and your attorney will have to respond to these requests unless they're grossly unreasonable; if you think they are unreasonable, you'll have to file your own legal papers asking the court to issue an order stating that you don't have to honor the requests. (Otherwise, you and your attorney may be subject to sanctions, possibly including dismissal of your case.)

The court you're suing in could also have an impact on how long your matter will take; for instance, a matter in small-claims court will most likely get a quick hearing date, whereas another court may have a two-year waiting list to get a trial date. Although your attorney may be able to give you estimates of the average amount of time a matter such as yours might take, often an accurate timetable estimate is not possible.

WHAT KINDS OF COURT APPEARANCES MUST I MAKE TO PURSUE THIS LAWSUIT?

In some simple cases, you may never have to set foot inside the courtroom. If your adversary owes you an exact sum of money and fails to appear (that is, put in legal papers defending his action), you may be able to get a judgment by default by having your attorney prepare papers describing the validity of your claim, having you sign them, and submitting these papers to the court.

However, if your adversary appears and serves you with a notice to take your deposition (oral testimony) before trial, you may have to appear in court or at an attorney's office before the trial begins to answer his attorney's questions about the details of your claim. After that, if your case goes to trial, you'll have to appear to testify, again, about the details of your claim.

Often, it's just not possible to predict if or how many times you may be asked to testify in court. Depending upon the type of court action you're pursuing, and whether or not your adversary "appears" in the action, you may or may not have to appear in court to obtain a judgment.

WHAT ARE MY COURT COSTS GOING TO BE?

Court costs are the actual out-of-pocket expenses (other than attorneys' fees) you will have to pay when starting a lawsuit, such as court filing fees, fees for service of process, investigation fees, and sheriff's fees. Laws vary from state to state as to what costs are and which can be reimbursed by your adversary if you win your lawsuit.

Court costs vary from state to state. Some possible costs might be as follows: hiring of process server, $25 for each person you are suing; purchasing index number from the court, $170; request to put case on the court calendar, $75; stenography fees in out-of-court depositions, $8 per page; investigation fees, $300 per day; fees to register your judgment in other counties, $15 per county; sheriff's fees, $15.

DO I GET REIMBURSED FOR COURT COSTS IF I WIN MY CASE?

All or some of the above-mentioned expenses may be reimbursed to you by your adversary if you win your lawsuit. For instance, although your actual expenses are much higher, you may be limited by law to a $500 reimbursement by your adversary if you are successful in your lawsuit. Your attorney will probably ask that you pay her money up front to cover out-of-pocket expenses since your reimbursement, if any, will only be made after the lawsuit is concluded.

WILL I BE ABLE TO RECOVER MY ATTORNEYS' FEES FROM MY ADVERSARY IF I WIN?

Generally, you will not be able to recover the attorneys' fees you spent to bring your lawsuit, unless your

contract provided for payment of attorneys' fees or if
payment of attorneys' fees is authorized by law for the
specific type of lawsuit you have brought.

If you're bringing a lawsuit for a matter such as sex discrimination, and the law under which you are suing
authorizes you to recover your attorney's fees from the
discriminator, you will be allowed to recover your attorneys' fees. However, if your neighbor willfully destroyed
all the lawn in your front yard by driving over it with his
four-wheel-drive vehicle, and there is no specific law in
your area that authorizes recovery of attorneys' fees, you
will not be able to recover your attorneys' fees when you
sue the neighbor for the damage.

Suppose you're suing over a breach of contract—you
loaned money to someone and your agreement provided
that in the event of default by the borrower, you, as the
lender, could recover your attorneys' fees. In this case, you
will be able to recover these costs. However, if the same
agreement said nothing on the issue of attorneys' fees, you
would not be able to recover them from the borrower. So,
when you enter into an agreement, ask your attorney
whether her fees will be automatically reimbursed if you
have to sue, or if you should include a clause in the agreement you're making to cover such a contingency.

IF I WIN MY LAWSUIT AND GET A JUDGMENT IN MY FAVOR, HOW LONG DOES THE JUDGMENT REMAIN VALID?

Each state has different laws that will tell you how long
your judgment is good for. For instance, your judgment
may be valid to enforce against other assets of your adversary for a period of twenty years after the judgment is filed.

Sometimes this period can be extended by filing
papers with the sheriff to "levy" upon (enforce your judgment against) assets of your adversary. For instance, if

after nineteen years and eleven months, you discover that your adversary has just inherited a large sum of money, you may be able to deliver papers to the sheriff that will allow you to go after the inheritance even though the twenty-year period is about to expire.

After your judgment expires, you can no longer collect the amount due, so knowing how long your judgment is good for and whether it can be extended are important facts.

IF I WIN MY LAWSUIT, WHAT ARE MY PROSPECTS OF COLLECTING A JUDGMENT IN MY FAVOR?

Coming out of work last week, you slipped and fell on the ice on the sidewalk of your office building. Should you sue? If the building maintains liability insurance for injury to persons using the building, you know there's a source of funds from which you can collect a possible judgment. However, if you decide to sue a nineteen-year-old unemployed youth with no assets who sent you to the hospital with a broken nose, you may not be able to find any source of funds from which you can collect your judgment even if you win the suit.

It doesn't make sense to spend time and effort pursuing a claim if there's no source of money available for you to collect from once you've won. Before you start a lawsuit, it's a good idea to conduct an investigation into the financial capacity of your prospective adversary to determine what your prospects of collecting a possible judgment are.

IF I WIN MY LAWSUIT AND GET A COURT JUDGMENT IN MY FAVOR, AND I KNOW THE MONEY'S AVAILABLE, HOW CAN I COLLECT IT?

Unfortunately, the losers in lawsuits are often uncooperative, and you must locate assets that you can legally seize and sell to collect the money due you.

Fortunately, there are various methods of collecting money owed to you. If you have copies of your adversary's checks, you can send legal papers to the bank where the account is located to restrain that account. That way no checks can be paid to others until your debt has been paid in full or the funds in the account exhausted. If you don't have copies of checks, you can send notices to all of the banks in your adversary's home town to find out whether there are any accounts in existence and, if so, to similarly restrain them.

If you have a judgment against your adversary's business, you can send the sheriff to shut the business down and sell the assets. You can search the land records of your locality to see if your adversary holds any real property in her name, and if so, you can file the judgment in that locality and then bring a proceeding to sell the real estate to pay off your judgment. In some states, you can send a notice to your adversary's employer to have the employer send you a percentage (fixed by law) of his paycheck until your judgment has been paid in full. The more you know about the finances of your adversary, the more options you and your attorney will have to collect money that is due you on a judgment. Each of these procedures may take time; there is no guarantee that you will get your money quickly.

IN ANOTHER STATE, THE CONTRACTOR I HIRED TO INSTALL A SWIMMING POOL IN MY COUNTRY HOUSE BROKE HIS AGREEMENT. I BROUGHT A LAWSUIT AGAINST HIM IN MY HOME STATE. THE COURT DISMISSED THE CASE BECAUSE THE JUDGE SAID I HAD BROUGHT THE LAWSUIT IN THE WRONG STATE. WHY CAN'T I SUE IN MY HOME STATE?

Although it may be convenient for you to sue in your home state on a claim that relates to an out-of-state matter, most courts will require that you start your lawsuit in the state most related to the incident.

In the example above, both your country home and the contractor were located in another state. Since, presumably, you enter the other state for the purposes of visiting your house, it would not be unfair to have you go into the out-of-state court to press your claim.

Suppose the out-of-state contractor solicited business in your home state, and you employed the contractor to do work on your in-state residence. If your contractor failed to complete the job properly, you could sue him in your own state. In this latter example, the contractor could not claim inconvenience, since he was the one who came to your home state to look for business from you.

I OBTAINED A JUDGMENT IN MY STATE AGAINST THE MANUFACTURER OF A DEFECTIVE WASHING MACHINE THAT BLEW UP IN MY FACE, CAUSING ME INJURY. HOWEVER, THE MANUFACTURER HAS ITS OFFICE AND ALL OF ITS ASSETS IN AN ADJOINING STATE. HOW CAN I ENFORCE MY JUDGMENT IN ANOTHER STATE?

Generally, you'll have to find an attorney who is qualified to practice law in the second state to have your judgment converted into a valid judgment there. (If your own attorney isn't qualified, he can help you locate a qualified lawyer in the second state.) The second state will not make you go through the entire lawsuit again, but will have you go through a simplified procedure to have your judgment recognized.

To enforce your judgment against the washing machine manufacturer, your attorney will probably have to prepare papers for you to sign verifying your claim and will also obtain a "certified" copy (copy with a court seal) of your original judgment to submit with the papers. Converting your judgment into one valid in another state will probably be a much quicker procedure than it was to get the judgment in the first place since you will not have to re-prove the liability of the washing machine manufacturer. Generally, you must only prove that you have a valid judgment from another state.

WHEN I STARTED A LAWSUIT AGAINST MY ADVERSARY, I KNEW THAT SHE HAD A LOT OF BANK ACCOUNTS IN HER NAME. HOWEVER, NOW THAT I HAVE THE JUDGMENT, THE BANK ADVISES ME THAT ALL OF THE MONEY HAS BEEN WITHDRAWN AND THE ACCOUNTS CLOSED. WHAT CAN I DO?

It's a common tactic for adversaries to try to hide or dissipate assets so that by the time a judgment is entered in a lawsuit, no visible assets are available. However, you have the right to take a postjudgment deposition of your adversary to find out where these funds went. (If she lies under oath, you can have her arrested for perjury.) If she tells you that she felt generous and gave all of her money away to her husband or to a friend, you may have the right to sue them both to recover these funds. To the extent you can trace her funds to others, you may be able to recover assets transferred to third parties to avoid paying you.

WHAT CAN I DO IF I DON'T AGREE WITH THE JUDGE'S DECISION OR THE JURY'S VERDICT IN MY CASE?

You may be entitled to an appeal of your case to a higher court if there is a valid reason why the case should be reviewed (for instance, if you think that the jury misinterpreted the evidence or if you think that the judge made an error in interpreting the law in your matter).

For example, the judge may have given the jury incorrect instruction at the trial. Instead of instructing the jury that you had no duty to help the stranger you had passed on the highway, perhaps the judge erroneously instructed the jury that you had a duty to stop and render medical aid to the stranger whom you saw injured on the side of the road. You could appeal to a higher court on the basis that the judge made an erroneous instruction under the law.

Suppose a jury made an error in addition and awarded you only $150,000 in a case where your evidence (bills and invoices) supported a claim of $200,000. This time you could appeal to a higher court because there was a mistake of fact.

MUST I APPEAL IMMEDIATELY IF I FEEL I WAS WRONGED?

You only have a limited time to appeal (say, perhaps, thirty days after a judgment is entered), so you and your attorney must decide quickly whether you want to try to appeal to a higher court, if one is available. A higher court may not be available if you've already appealed to the highest court in your state, and the Supreme Court of the United States in Washington, D.C., has declined to hear your case. (The United States Supreme Court only has a limited number of cases they will hear, and they often pick the ones they feel have the most impact on the rest of the country.)

I WAS JUST SERVED WITH LEGAL PAPERS STATING THAT I'M BEING SUED. WHAT DO I DO?

You should contact an attorney as soon as possible, since procedural deadlines come into effect as soon as you receive the papers. For instance, if legal papers in an action for a divorce by your husband are personally delivered to you, you may have only twenty days to serve a formal, written response on your adversary. If legal papers in the same divorce action were received by you other than by handing them to you directly, you may have additional time (perhaps thirty days instead of twenty) in which to make your written response. In any case, you should not ignore legal papers that have been served upon you, or you may risk losing legal rights as you let the deadlines pass by.

I JUST FOUND A COPY OF LEGAL PAPERS ADDRESSED TO ME LYING UNDERNEATH THE BUSHES OUTSIDE MY HOUSE. I KNOW THAT THE PAPERS WERE NOT PROPERLY SERVED ON ME ACCORDING TO THE LAWS OF MY STATE. SINCE THE PAPERS WERE NOT PROPERLY SERVED, DO I HAVE TO DO ANYTHING?

If you find legal papers, but you think they were improperly served upon you, you must not ignore them, or the person who started the lawsuit against you may be entitled to get a judgment by default against you.

If you don't formally respond to the legal papers, your adversary will have the right to petition the court to enter a judgment against you in your absence, even if you may have a valid defense against the action.

Suppose you accidentally bounce a check against someone because of a bank error. Even though you have a valid defense to the court action, if you don't respond to the court papers, your adversary will be able to get a judgment against you in the amount of his claim, and it will have the same effect (your adversary will be able to seize your assets) as if you fought the lawsuit and lost.

ALTHOUGH I NEVER RECEIVED ANY LEGAL PAPERS TO NOTIFY ME OF A LAWSUIT AGAINST ME, THE SHERIFF JUST CAME TO MY HOME AND SERVED ME WITH PAPERS STATING THAT A JUDGMENT HAS BEEN ENTERED AGAINST ME. WHAT SHOULD I DO?

Don't panic. If you find that a judgment has been entered against you without your knowledge, you may be entitled to go to court to have the judgment "vacated" (that is, canceled in the court records).

What if the above-mentioned sheriff delivers you papers stating that your credit card company has a judgment against you, but you never received notice of the lawsuit? If you have a valid defense (such as the amount they were suing you for was under dispute), and if you act within the amount of time specified in your local law (for instance, one year), your attorney will be able to petition the court on your behalf to have the judgment vacated.

If you don't have a valid defense to the lawsuit (for instance, you didn't pay your credit card bill because you were angry at an employee of the credit card company), you may not be entitled to have the judgment canceled, depending upon your local law. Or, if you don't act within the prescribed time, you may also be unable to have the judgment set aside. Ask the right questions if something like this happens to you, or else you may lose substantial rights.

IF I'M SERVED WITH LEGAL PAPERS AND BROUGHT INTO A LAWSUIT, AND I THINK SOMEONE ELSE IS RESPONSIBLE FOR THE PROBLEM, CAN I SERVE LEGAL PAPERS ON THEM TO COMPEL THEM TO PARTICIPATE IN THE LAWSUIT?

Yes. Suppose you are in a car accident involving three vehicles. The driver of car two sues you for damages to him and his car. You think car three caused the crash by failing to stop at a red light. You can serve the driver and owner of car three with legal papers to force them into your lawsuit.

I AM A TENANT IN AN APARTMENT BUILDING. MY LAND-LORD IS SUING ME FOR NONPAYMENT OF RENT. I STOPPED PAYING THE RENT BECAUSE THERE WAS A FLOOD FROM A DEFECTIVE SPRINKLER SYSTEM, WHICH HAS DAMAGED ALL OF MY CLOTHES, FURNITURE, AND ELECTRONIC EQUIPMENT. CAN I MAKE A CLAIM FOR DAMAGE TO MY PERSONAL THINGS IN THE SAME LAWSUIT?

If someone starts a lawsuit against you, you have the right to counterclaim for monetary damage or any other relief related to the original claim. In the above example, since the landlord's duty to provide you with a dry apartment has been breached, you can claim the resulting damages to your clothes, furniture, and electronic equipment to offset the amount you owed to him as rent (provided there is not a clause in your lease agreeing to pay the rent whether or not the premises are habitable).

A CLIENT OF MINE OWES ME $850 FOR ACCOUNTING SER-VICES I RENDERED TO HIM. MY ATTORNEY SAYS THAT IT WOULD BE TOO EXPENSIVE FOR ME TO HIRE HIM TO BRING A LAWSUIT ON MY BEHALF, BUT THAT I COULD PURSUE THE MATTER MYSELF IN SMALL-CLAIMS COURT. IS SMALL-CLAIMS COURT A GOOD CHOICE FOR ME?

If you have a small claim for money damages only (such as a client not paying you for services rendered), small-claims court can be an excellent choice.

Small-claims court usually has a low monetary "ceiling," such as $2,000. You don't need an attorney to file your claim, and the filing fees are usually significantly lower than those in other courts (such as $35 instead of $175). The case is usually scheduled on the court calendar for several weeks after you file your claim, so you will not have to wait as long as you might in other courts. The court rules are more relaxed, so you don't have to be a procedural expert to manage your own case.

However, small-claims court may not be able to handle every type of small case. If you're seeking return of your prize pig because the purchaser's check bounced, the court may not have the power to issue orders to compel the return of property (as opposed to money). Also, if the amount of your claim exceeds the court's money limit, you'll be restricted in your recovery to the court's limit.

I AM AN ANESTHESIOLOGIST. THE SURGEON WITH WHOM I JUST PERFORMED A BONE REPAIR OPERATION AND I WERE JUST SUED BY THE PATIENT, WHO DEVELOPED A POSTOPERATIVE INFECTION. THE SURGEON OWES ME MONEY FROM SOME MEDICAL PRODUCTS I JUST SOLD TO HIM. CAN I MAKE A CLAIM AGAINST THE SURGEON FOR THE MONEY HE OWES ME NOW THAT WE ARE IN THE SAME LAWSUIT, OR MUST I START MY OWN LAWSUIT?

Although our court systems encourage bringing all of the proper parties into one action for resolution of a dispute, the courts will either discourage or prohibit litigants from bringing in a separate dispute, unrelated to the original claim, which does not involve all of the parties in the lawsuit.

In this example, even though the issue of payment for the medical products contract involves two parties in the same lawsuit, it is totally unrelated to the original claim for personal injury and is of no concern to the original claimant. Therefore, the court will most likely refuse to allow the separate claim to be interposed in the lawsuit and will insist that any claim on the contract be resolved by a separate lawsuit between the surgeon and the anesthesiologist. However, it is best to let your attorney know about all possible claims you may have against any of the parties because some courts may require such joinder.

If all the parties in the lawsuit were involved in this unrelated claim, the court may agree to hear both claims in the same lawsuit. For example, if the patient happened to be the manufacturer of the medical products, which the surgeon claims are defective, the court may agree to hear the contract dispute in the same lawsuit as the personal injury action.

SECTION 7

BUSTED: SMART QUESTIONS TO ASK ABOUT CRIMINAL LAW

Most of us are law-abiding citizens with no intentions of any wrongdoing. But life is full of surprises, and you never know when you may be suspected—rightly or wrongly—of doing something that is not only against your nature, but against the law as well.

Don't wait until you're in trouble to read this section of the book. You may never need to know the answers to the questions that follow; but if you do, it's better to know them before you're arrested than after.

When you're in trouble, it's more important than ever that you remain calm and able to think. Questions stimulate thought. Ask yourself questions (what really happened at the scene of the crime, who might have seen it, did the police act properly, etc.). Ask your lawyer questions. Get her thinking about all the possible options for your defense. This is no time to be passive and let someone else "take care of everything."

That doesn't mean you are belligerent or have a bad attitude. It means that you're fighting for your rights, and possibly your freedom, so no stone should be left unturned.

You'll never be 100 percent free of fear and anxiety if you're in trouble with the law. You can't be your own judge or your own jury. But you can take charge of your own education and attitude. The more you learn about your case and about the law, the less anxious you'll be. The less anxiety you have, the better your chances of going in with a positive attitude and coming out with justice served.

I'VE WATCHED ENOUGH TELEVISION TO KNOW THAT IF I'M ARRESTED FOR A CRIME, I SHOULD CALL MY ATTORNEY. THE POLICE TOLD ME I CAN DO THAT WHEN WE GET TO THE POLICE STATION. WHAT SHOULD I DO IN THE MEANTIME?

Stay calm, but don't expect that everything you experience will be just as you've seen it on "L.A. Law" or "Perry Mason." You'll probably be upset and you may be in a state of confusion after you are arrested. But there are a few things you can (and should) do to preserve your rights under the law and assist your attorney in preparing the best possible defense for you.

First, ask the arresting officer what crime you're being charged with if he or she hasn't already told you. Even if you think you're innocent, don't argue with the police officers. Concentrate instead on recalling as many details as possible about the incident that prompted the arrest.

If you're arrested at the "crime" scene, check to see if there are any witnesses to the incident. Get a good picture in your mind of the physical condition of the area of the alleged crime. If you notice someone carrying something away from the scene before the police arrived, or any other unusual behavior, remember the details so you can later tell your attorney.

It's best to call an attorney as soon as possible after you are arrested. Even if you're arrested for what you believe to be a minor offense, you may have underestimated the possible consequences. If you don't have an attorney, a public defender will be assigned to you.

Although the police officers may ask you questions, you should advise them that you will not answer any questions about the crime unless your attorney is present. "You have the right to remain silent" should have been one of the rights you were advised of at the time of arrest; keep this right in mind—"anything you say can and will be used against you in a court of law."

HOW LONG CAN I BE DETAINED BY THE POLICE AFTER I'M ARRESTED?

This depends on the type of crime you're accused of and on your local laws. You may be issued an "appearance ticket" and released almost immediately; you may have to await arraignment and fixing of bail; or you may be incarcerated without bail until after your trial is concluded.

WHAT IS AN APPEARANCE TICKET?

If you're accused of a less-serious type of misdemeanor (such as spraying graffiti on someone's sidewalk), the police officer assigned to your case may have the option of issuing an "appearance ticket," which is similar to a traffic court summons. This would require your appearance for arraignment in court at a later date, without having to post any bail.

WHAT IS AN ARRAIGNMENT?

If you're not given an appearance ticket, you must wait in police custody until you are arraigned, or formally charged with a crime. Depending upon your area and the time of the day you were "picked up," you may or may not be arraigned the same day. (In some courts, judges may be "on call" twenty-four hours a day to handle arraignments, but in other courts they may only be available during certain hours, such as 7:00 A.M. to 11:00 P.M.)

WHAT RIGHTS DO I HAVE AT AN ARRAIGNMENT?

At the arraignment you'll be advised of your rights, including the right to be represented by counsel, the right to the adjournment of the arraignment in order to retain counsel, the right to have counsel appointed for you if you're not able to afford an attorney, and the right to separate counsel for codefendants (persons accused of committing the crime with you).

If you don't have an attorney at the time of arraignment and want to get one, you can ask for a postponement until you can get an attorney, either on your own or from the public defender's office. (You will remain in custody while you get an attorney unless you have posted the required bail, if any.)

At the arraignment, the criminal charges will be read aloud to you. You have the right to get a copy of the criminal complaint specifying the charges against you; if it has not already been given to you, your attorney will ask for a copy of the charges at this time. If your attorney already has a copy of the charges, she or he will ask to "waive" (dispense with) reading of the charges. This will save you the public embarrassment of everyone else in the courtroom knowing the charges brought against you (such as child abuse of your nephew).

WHAT HAPPENS IF I PLEAD GUILTY AT THE ARRAIGNMENT?

If you enter a plea of guilty, the arraignment judge may sentence you right away or schedule sentencing at a later date.

WHAT HAPPENS IF I PLEAD NOT GUILTY AT THE ARRAIGNMENT?

Your attorney will demand that the prosecuting attorney furnish a copy of the records of the police and the prosecutor's office as to the particulars of the alleged crime, and the case will continue.

After you've pleaded not guilty to the charges, the judge may release you without fixing bail—either on your own recognizance (that is, without court supervision) or with a duty on your part to report to a probation officer at periodic intervals. The judge could impose bail which you must post or remain in police custody until your trial. If you're accused of a serious crime (such as murder of a police officer), the judge may require that you be held without opportunity of bail due to the nature of the crime. If this is the case, you'll be held by the police until after your trial is concluded.

WHAT FACTORS WILL THE COURT CONSIDER WHEN DECIDING WHETHER I SHOULD BE RELEASED OR WHETHER BAIL WILL BE FIXED (AND FOR HOW MUCH)?

The judge wants to ensure your presence at all of your court hearings, including your trial. If you and your attorney can convince the judge that you will, in fact, appear at these proceedings without the necessity of posting bail and that you will not be a danger to the community between the time of arraignment and the time of trial, you may be released.

Your "roots in the community" will be a significant factor in assessing whether or not you will appear at your criminal proceedings. Also, the seriousness of the crime, and your prior criminal record, if any, will be considered in determining whether you might be a danger to the public.

Here are the facts: You are accused of shoplifting a $100 jacket from a local store. You hold a regular job in a car wash, live with your law-abiding mother in the area, and have no prior record of criminal behavior. In this case, the judge will probably release you on your bare promise to return when you are supposed to.

However, if you're a drug dealer accused of killing a police officer while committing a robbery and have three prior convictions for assault, it's highly unlikely that you will be released on your own. More likely the judge will fix either a high amount of bail or no bail at all.

WHAT CAN I DO IF I THINK MY BAIL IS EXCESSIVE?

If you and your attorney think the bail is excessive, your attorney should immediately make a request before the court to have the amount of the bail lowered. If you're accused of your first offense of driving while intoxicated, and the judge set bail at $20,000, your attorney should plead for a reduction in bail. If the court persists in its refusal to lower the amount of bail, your attorney may immediately apply to have the amount of bail reviewed by a nonjudicial agency. Such an agency may monitor the bail amounts fixed by certain judges in certain types of cases, and if a judge shows a pattern of fixing excessive bail, they may have the authority to have the amount of bail reduced or the judge censured.

AFTER THE ARRAIGNMENT, WHAT HAPPENS NEXT?

Your attorney will request a conference with the prosecuting attorney and possibly the judge to discuss what your options are in resolving your case. This may take some time, as your attorney will need a chance to become totally familiar with your case and to research the applicable law in your case so that he or she can recommend the best option for you.

One option might be to plead guilty to a lesser version of the crime in exchange for a recommendation by the prosecutor of a more lenient sentence. (Most convictions are based upon these kinds of pleas rather than upon verdicts after trial by jury.) For instance, if you're accused of committing robbery in the first degree, which carries a maximum jail sentence of ten years, you may be able to negotiate with the prosecutor to plead guilty to robbery in the third degree, which only carries a maximum sentence of five years.

Or, if you're accused of driving while under the influence of drugs or alcohol, which carries a maximum one-year jail sentence, you may be able to plead guilty to a lesser charge of driving while impaired, which may carry a maximum prison term of ninety days (which you may have a good chance of having suspended if this is your first offense).

However, if you believe you're not guilty of the accused crime, you may wish to wait for a trial, at which time you'll have the right to present your case to a jury of your peers.

WILL I ALWAYS BE ENTITLED TO A JURY TRIAL IN MY CRIMINAL CASE?

You are entitled to be tried by a jury of your peers if you are accused of committing a crime. As in civil (noncriminal) cases, you and your attorney may decide, strategywise, that you may prefer not to have a trial by jury in certain cases.

Suppose you were the general contractor on a building that collapsed and killed several people because you (allegedly) intentionally and knowingly used improper materials to construct the building. You're accused of criminally negligent homicide. The testimony you will introduce in your defense will come from technical experts who'll show how the concrete mix you used had the exact structural properties specified in the architect's plans. Due to the technical nature of the testimony, you may prefer to have your case heard by a judge, whose level of education may exceed those persons selected in a general jury and whom you feel will more fully comprehend the details of your defense.

HOW LONG MUST I WAIT BEFORE MY CASE GOES TO TRIAL?

Unlike a civil case, where it may take you years to get on the court calendar to have a trial, in a criminal case you're guaranteed a "speedy" trial. Depending upon the severity of the crime, your local laws will specify the time period within which your case must be tried.

In a felony case (such as murder), your local law might specify that your case must go to trial within one year after the date you were arrested or arraigned. In a misdemeanor case (such as theft of a small amount of money) where you're likely to be released on your own recognizance or where the bail set is low, the law may specify that a trial within two years is considered to be "speedy."

If there's no bail set, or you can't pay the bail, it's possible that you will remain in jail during this waiting period. If you do, this time is included in your eventual jail sentence.

WHAT HAPPENS IF THE TRIAL IS NOT STARTED WITHIN THE PRESCRIBED TIME?

If it is due to the fault (or inaction) of the prosecutor, you may make a motion to have your case dismissed. However, all prosecutors are well aware of the deadlines, and few cases pass beyond the time limits.

If any delay was caused by you or your attorney before your case goes to trial (such as requests for adjournments by you), this time is not counted when computing the time within which the trial must begin. For instance, if your attorney requested an adjournment of the trial in order to procure additional evidence, the speedy trial time would be extended by the amount of the requested time.

WHAT ARE THE LEGAL DEFENSES TO THE CRIME I AM ACCUSED OF COMMITTING?

You may have defenses that can acquit (absolve) you of legal accountability for that crime. Suppose a large person was running at you waving a sharp knife in his hand, shouting that he was going to kill you. Suppose you drew your (legally registered) gun and killed that person. You won't be convicted of murder if you can convince the jury and the judge that you acted in self-defense.

What if you intended only to burglarize someone's house, but caused the occupant to have a heart attack when she tried to chase you down the hall with her great-grandfather's Civil War saber? You won't be convicted of intentional murder if you can prove you had no weapons and were fleeing the residence at the time.

Or perhaps you were on leave from a mental asylum and robbed a woman on the street of her wallet. If you can prove that you were mentally incapable of having criminal intent, you can be acquitted of the crime.

You should ask your attorney what your available defenses are, and what the chances of convincing a jury of the truth of your defenses are. (Remember, any defenses are useless unless the jury believes you!)

ARE THERE ANY FLAWS IN THE PROSECUTOR'S CASE THAT WILL WORK IN MY FAVOR?

The prosecutor has to prove beyond a reasonable doubt that a crime was committed and that you are the one (or one of the ones) who did it. If any of the state's evidence against you on either of these issues can be disproved or barred from being presented at trial, this helps you, as the defendant, to weaken the state's case against you.

You're accused of possession of cocaine, for example. If you can prove that it was found while the police were conducting an illegal search of your home (perhaps without a proper search warrant or without probable cause), you'll be able to exclude evidence obtained during that search at your trial. If the cocaine obtained as a result of the illegal search was the only evidence against you, your case will probably be dismissed before it even goes to trial, since there will be no admissible evidence that a crime was even committed.

Now suppose you're suspected of committing a robbery. The only evidence is that the victim picked you out of an illegally conducted police lineup. Although there may be evidence that a crime was committed, the prosecutor may have no legally obtained evidence that you were the one who did it. The state's case against you may therefore be flawed.

IF I HAVE A VALID DEFENSE OR IF THERE IS A FLAW IN THE PROSECUTOR'S CASE, DO I HAVE TO WAIT FOR A TRIAL, OR CAN MY ATTORNEY TRY TO GET THE CASE DISMISSED AHEAD OF TIME?

Your attorney can try to have the charges against you dropped at a conference with the prosecutor (and possibly the judge) prior to trial, at the time plea negotiations are conducted. If this doesn't work, your attorney can file "motion" papers formally requesting that the court rule on these issues in advance of trial or that the charges against you be dismissed in their entirety prior to trial. The motion papers will contain affidavits from persons having knowledge of the facts of the case and probably a memorandum of law setting forth (for the judge) the applicable law in such a situation. The prosecutor's office will submit papers in opposition to your motion, and then the judge will decide if you're entitled to the relief you are requesting.

WHAT IS THE PUNISHMENT I CAN RECEIVE IF I AM CONVICTED?

Generally, the more serious the crime is, the longer and/or more severe the punishment will be. Your local law will specify the maximum sentence (and, if applicable, any minimum sentence) for the crime you are accused of committing.

For minor crimes, a fine and/or short jail sentence may be the maximum allowable punishment. For a first offense of driving while intoxicated, for instance, the maximum sentence may be one year of incarceration. However, for more serious crimes, a lengthy jail term or even the death penalty (in some states only) may be mandatory if you are convicted. If this is your second or third conviction of murder while committing a robbery, the sentence may be a maximum of life imprisonment.

WHAT'S THE DIFFERENCE BETWEEN CONCURRENT AND CONSECUTIVE SENTENCES?

If you're accused of several different crimes by reason of the same incident (for instance, kidnapping and subsequent murder of your victim) or committing the same crime against multiple victims (such as gunning down ten people in a shoot-out), the judge has the right to give you a full sentence for each of the crimes you are convicted of. The judge may give you ten years' imprisonment for kidnapping and ten years' imprisonment for murder.

The judge will then decree if the sentences are to run concurrently (meaning that they all start running at the same time) or consecutively (meaning that one full sentence runs out, and then the next one starts, and so on). If the two ten-year sentences are to run concurrently, then you may have to serve a maximum sentence of ten years for the two crimes. If the two ten-year sentences are to run consecutively, you may have to serve a maximum of twenty years for the two crimes. The actual amount of time you serve will depend upon whether the judge gives you the maximum sentence allowable under the law and whether you become eligible for parole at an earlier date.

IF I AM CONVICTED AND SENTENCED, HOW AND WHEN WILL I BECOME ELIGIBLE FOR PAROLE?

In most cases you'll be entitled to apply for parole in advance of serving the full term of your sentence. If you're given a nine-year jail sentence for embezzling funds from your employer, for instance, you may be eligible for parole in three years, according to your local law. The judge who sentences you may have the discretionary power to deny the opportunity of parole to you, depending upon the circumstances of the crime. If you've been convicted of committing a mass murder of persons attending religious services, the judge may decree that you serve a life sentence in jail, without opportunity of parole. However, if you have been convicted of the murder of your lover in the "heat of passion," you may be given a life sentence with the opportunity to apply for parole after serving fifteen years.

CAN I BE FORCED TO TESTIFY AGAINST MYSELF AT MY OWN TRIAL?

No, you can't. The state has the burden of proving beyond a reasonable doubt that you committed a crime. If you and your attorney feel that the state has a weak case, you may choose not to testify and just let the state's case fail on its own or be disproved by other evidence you may submit (for instance, testimony of witnesses at the scene).

If you do choose to testify at your trial, you can be cross-examined by the prosecutor, who might try to get you to contradict what you said, or to impeach your credibility as a witness (for instance, by showing that you previously lied under oath). So you and your attorney may decide it's better strategy not to testify.

WHAT ABOUT "TAKING THE FIFTH"?

You have the ultimate right to invoke the Fifth Amendment to the United States Constitution by refusing to incriminate yourself. The jury does not have the right to infer anything from the fact that you decline to testify, so the fact that you do so decline cannot be formally used against you. However, many defense attorneys feel that it's better not to testify at all than to make people think you have something to hide by refusing to answer questions on the witness stand.

IF I'M SUSPECTED OF COMMITTING A CRIME, CAN THE POLICE FORCE ME TO PARTICIPATE IN A LINEUP AT THE POLICE STATION?

If there was an "eyewitness" to the crime, the police want to make sure it was you she saw. Upon proper notice by the prosecutor to your attorney, you can be compelled to participate in a lineup for the purposes of having the purported witness try to identify you as the suspect in the case.

The lineup must be properly conducted by the police. The other people in the lineup should be of similar age and physical appearance. For instance, if you are a white man and all the other men in the lineup are black, you'll be able to have the results of the lineup identification suppressed due to dissimilarity in appearance of the possible choices.

The police will usually take a picture of all the candidates in the lineup so if any future question as to the fairness of the lineup is contested, there will be evidence available to document the event. Your attorney will most likely bring along a witness to attend the lineup so that if testimony has to be given (for instance, about any conversation held during the lineup), a third party will be available to testify.

CAN MY SPOUSE DIVORCE ME IF I AM CONVICTED OF A CRIME AND MUST SERVE A JAIL SENTENCE?

Depending upon the laws of your particular state, your spouse may have the right to divorce you if you are in prison. If you're incarcerated for a period of twenty years to life for murdering your former employer for firing you from your job, your wife may have the right to divorce you under local law, because you have been convicted of a felony and must serve an extended jail sentence. However, your spouse may not have a similar right if you're convicted of a less serious crime.

WHAT HAPPENS TO MY PROPERTY IF I AM CONVICTED OF A CRIME AND MUST SERVE A JAIL SENTENCE?

Unless there is a specific law that provides that your property will be confiscated if you are convicted of a particular crime, you generally retain your property rights if you must serve a prison term.

When you're admitted into jail, your personal belongings will be stored for safekeeping but returned to you upon your release. However, some federal and state laws provide for confiscation of property of a convicted felon that was used in connection with a crime. For example, if you used your home as the center for an organized crime syndicate that distributed heroin throughout the area, and you are convicted of violation of federal anti-organized crime laws, the prosecutor can apply to the court to have your home confiscated, sold, and the proceeds turned over to the federal government.

Similarly, if you hold several bank accounts, the money in these accounts will continue to be held in your name and accrue interest or dividends while you are in jail—unless the money in those accounts was obtained by your criminal acts, in which case a court order may be issued directing that these funds be returned to the person from whom you took the money.

WHILE I AM IN PRISON, WILL ANY OF MY CIVIL RIGHTS BE LOST OR SUSPENDED?

While you are in prison, certain of your civil rights may be affected, and these laws will vary from state to state. For instance, your right to vote in political elections may be temporarily suspended while you are in jail.

DO I NEED TO CALL AN ATTORNEY IF I AM STOPPED FOR A MINOR TRAFFIC VIOLATION?

Even if you're stopped for what you believe to be a minor offense and issued only a ticket, it may pay to call an attorney as soon as possible after the event, since you may have overlooked or underestimated the possible consequences of the incident.

Take a case where you're stopped for driving an automobile in excess of the speed limit, but you believe you're innocent. This is your first such incident. You may not think it's very serious; however, your automobile insurance carrier may consider it in computing your next year's automobile insurance rates. Conviction of this offense, even if it means only paying a fine, could result in an increase in your insurance premiums. If you are already in a high-risk insurance group (for instance, under age twenty-five), you may find that even after one ticket, your rates will go up. If you have a valid defense to the accused violation, the money you pay to an attorney to fight the ticket may be well worth it, since you may save on future insurance premiums. You always have the right to defend yourself.

On the other hand, if you're stopped for speeding for the third time in six months, the consequences may be more serious. The laws of your local jurisdiction may provide that your driver's license can be suspended or revoked if you are found guilty, even though for the prior events you got away with only paying a fine. If you need to drive an automobile to work, this could be a mere inconvenience; however, if you drive for a living, this could mean the loss of your job. And if your livelihood is at stake, you should involve an attorney at an early stage in the proceedings as opposed to after your license has been suspended so all of your rights can be protected. And you should stop speeding.

IF I'M A PEDESTRIAN WALKING ALONG THE STREET, DO THE POLICE HAVE A RIGHT TO DETAIN AND QUESTION ME?

If a police officer suspects a misdemeanor or a felony has been committed (for instance, someone in a fast-food restaurant just ran out and yelled, "Stop thief"), the officer can stop you and ask you for your name, address, and an explanation (for instance, where did you come from and where are you going?). If your explanation does not show some evidence of criminality—if you just bought takeout food from the restaurant, and you show the officer a paper bag filled with burgers—the officer has no right to detain you.

What if, instead of answering the officer's questions, you reach into the inside pocket of your coat? The officer might think you're about to pull out a weapon and may forceably stop you and search your person, since he has reason to suspect he's in danger of serious physical injury.

If, while searching for weapons, the officer discovers a large wad of cash in your coat pocket and has reasonable cause to believe that you robbed the fast-food restaurant (a person on the scene points at you and says, "She's the one"), the officer can arrest you on suspicion of having committed that crime.

IF I'M THE DRIVER OF AN AUTOMOBILE, DO THE POLICE HAVE THE RIGHT TO STOP AND DETAIN ME?

Stopping an automobile "substantially interferes" with your mobility and is considered a "seizure," which cannot be conducted by the police unless they have reasonable suspicion that something is wrong.

If a police officer observes your car weaving all over the road at 2:00 A.M. on New Year's Day, she would have reason to suspect that you might be driving while impaired and would have the right to stop your car.

If the smell of marijuana is evident in your car, and the officer observes you pushing a container under your seat, she can search both your car and the container. The smell of marijuana and your evasive behavior give probable cause to believe that you're in possession of the drug.

If, however, you air out the car and successfully hide the container of marijuana before the officer stops your car, she can't legally conduct a search of your car or the contents of any closed containers unless there are other events that might give her reasonable cause to search.

For instance, if the police officer observed you leaving a convicted drug dealer's house with a brown paper bag, she could follow you, stop your car, and search the brown paper bag without a warrant, even if she had no reason to search the car.

WHAT IF I'M A PASSENGER IN A CAR THAT HAS BEEN STOPPED BY THE POLICE. DO THEY HAVE THE RIGHT TO DETAIN AND QUESTION ME?

If the police lawfully stop the car (that is, the officers have reasonable suspicion to believe that something was wrong), they can treat you as if you're a pedestrian on the street.

So, as a passenger, if an officer suspects a misdemeanor or a felony has been committed (for instance, the car you are riding in meets the description of the getaway car in a local robbery), the police officer has the right to ask you your name, address, and an explanation of what happened. If there is no evidence against you of criminality, the officer does not have the right to go any further in questioning or detaining you.

However, if your car matches the description of the getaway car, both you and the driver are wearing black gloves and ski masks, and there is a pile of assorted dollar bills in the backseat of the car, the investigating officer has probable cause to suspect you and the driver had committed the robbery.

WHAT IS A GRAND JURY?

A grand jury decides if you should be indicted for a crime. For instance, if you hit (and killed) someone while driving your car, a grand jury could decide that since the person ran out between two parked cars and you were not speeding, the death was purely accidental. Or the grand jury could decide that there is reason to believe you were intoxicated at the time and should therefore stand trial.

Since a grand-jury proceeding can only result in an indictment (and not conviction) of a crime, your rights are different than if you have been arrested for a crime. Ask your attorney to explain them to you.

MY FOURTEEN-YEAR-OLD SON IS ACCUSED OF COMMITTING A CRIME. CAN HE BE TRIED, CONVICTED, AND SENTENCED AS AN ADULT?

Depending upon the laws of your state and the crime your son is accused of committing, he may or may not be treated as an adult for the crime he has committed.

Your state may have a law stating that all persons under age fifteen will be treated as children, possibly in family court instead of criminal court. There may be another category for children ages sixteen through nineteen within which your child may be eligible to be treated as a "youthful offender" in criminal court, unless he commits a serious felony, such as armed robbery or rape. If he is treated as a "youthful offender," he may appear at a trial before a judge only (not a jury), and the results may be noted as a finding only and not considered to be a conviction of a crime. Records of youthful offenders are normally confidential.

Just because your son falls into a certain age category doesn't mean he is automatically entitled to receive youthful-offender treatment. This depends on such factors as kind of crime, prior conviction of a felony as an adult, previous finding as a youthful offender, and whether the "interest of justice" will be served by affording him the protection of youthful-offender status.

DO I HAVE A DUTY TO REPORT A CRIME IF I WITNESS ONE?

Although morally and ethically you may feel a duty to report a crime if you see one, you may not have a legal obligation to inform the police. There are special categories of persons who by law have a legal duty to report a crime. A physician, licensed social worker, or registered nurse, may have a legal duty to report a suspected case of child abuse to the police. Similarly, a police officer, either on or off duty, may have a legal obligation to officially report a crime and may have the further duty to pursue the suspect.

However, if you're an ordinary citizen and you see some possible unlawful behavior, you have no duty to report it to the authorities, and no one can prosecute you under the criminal law system or the civil law system for failing to take any action.

DO I HAVE A LEGAL DUTY TO STOP A CRIME I OBSERVE IN PROGRESS?

Generally, if you have no legal duty to report a crime you observe, you have no duty to attempt to stop a crime you observe in progress. As a private citizen, you do not have a duty to thwart a crime as it happens.

However, if a police officer specifically commands you to assist her by holding a gun on a suspect she's apprehended at a crime scene, you might be compelled by local law to assist if asked to do so while a crime is in progress.

I HAVE BEEN THE VICTIM OF A CRIME. I KNOW THAT CRIME SUSPECTS HAVE RIGHTS. WHAT RIGHTS DO I HAVE?

If you have been injured, either bodily or by monetary loss, you may be entitled to compensation for your loss from either the perpetrator or from a victims' assistance bureau, if one exists in your area.

For instance, if someone is convicted of destroying your home by arson, the criminal court may be empowered to issue a fine against the convicted felon (in addition to the jail term) to compensate you for the loss of your house. Or you may be entitled to apply for a monetary award from the victims' assistance bureau, if a fund for such purposes has been set up in your state.

As a victim of a crime, you may also apply for the right to have your name withheld from the public while the trial on your matter is being held. If you have been the victim of a rape, the prosecutor can apply to the court to have your anonymity preserved before, during, and after the trial. You may also be able to secure psychological counseling after the crime from public agencies if the crime has caused you psychic injury (as many crimes do). Check with your local police department to inquire what services may be available to you.

SECTION 8

YOU AND THE CONSTITUTION: SMART QUESTIONS TO ASK ABOUT CIVIL RIGHTS

When this country was founded, it was designed to be a place where freedom reigned. From the very first settlers to the millions who have since come to these shores, America represents escape from religious and/or political oppression.

The Constitution was set up to guarantee freedom from oppression. Freedom never comes without a price, however. You cannot exercise your rights at the cost of someone else's. The First Amendment says you have the right to free speech, but the laws of our society say that you can't yell "fire" in a crowded room unless there actually is one.

In the best of all possible worlds, everyone is treated equally, no matter what their race, gender, color, religion, or political views. America is a great country, but it is not yet the best of all possible worlds. Therefore, laws

185

have been set up (and many more are needed) to be sure that all people are given equal access to the basic rights of making a living, securing shelter, and living with respect and dignity.

With our inalienable rights come great responsibilities. It's your responsibility to know your rights. If you think you're being discriminated against, find out what the laws are. You can consult an attorney, or you can get assistance from many local and federal government agencies. When you stand up for your own personal rights, you stand up for the rights of all people.

WHAT ARE MY CIVIL RIGHTS?

Your civil rights include freedom of religion, freedom of speech, freedom of expression, freedom of the press, freedom of association, the right to privacy, the right of personal liberty, freedom from discrimination by reason of race, color, religion, sex, or national origin, and the right to vote. Some of these rights are guaranteed to you by reason of the Constitution of the United States of America (and its amendments); others of these rights are guaranteed to you by reason of federal or state laws.

HOW DO I KNOW IF MY CIVIL RIGHTS HAVE BEEN VIOLATED?

Sometimes it's not easy to know when your rights are violated. For instance, if the cooperative apartment board where you want to live tells you they're rejecting your application because you're a Roman Catholic and they don't allow Roman Catholics to live in the building, your civil rights have obviously been violated.

However, sometimes the discrimination or violation is more subtle. Suppose your employer repeatedly asks you out for social dates. He makes no improper suggestions, but keeps asking you out. You tactfully refuse each time. When promotion time comes around, although you are the perfect candidate to fill the position, your subordinate gets the job instead of you. You may be a victim of sexual discrimination, even though your employer did not make the obvious advances one might expect.

HOW DO I PROTECT MYSELF AGAINST DISCRIMINATION?

Often, there is little you can do to "protect" yourself against discrimination. However, by becoming aware of your civil rights under the law, you'll be in a better position to know when your rights are being violated and when to seek appropriate legal redress.

For instance, if you suspect your employer is discriminating against you because of your national origin, you can call the Equal Employment Opportunity Commission at 1-800-872-3362 for further information. Most likely, there will be attorneys in your area specializing in employment discrimination who can evaluate your case and advise you whether, under your circumstances, you have a valid discrimination claim.

HOW DO I KNOW IF I HAVE A VALID DISCRIMINATION CLAIM?

The facts of your case will determine whether you have a valid claim. Suppose you are sixty-year-old waitress. You do your job well, yet you're fired with no explanation. Two weeks later, you find out that your replacement is twenty-three years old. You may have a claim under the federal Age Discrimination in Employment Act.

If the restaurant has fewer than twenty employees,

though, you may be out of luck, since the law currently covers establishments with twenty or more employees. However, your state or local law may cover your situation; check with an attorney or call your local government employment office to find out what you can do.

WHAT DO I DO IF I THINK MY CONSTITUTIONAL RIGHTS HAVE BEEN VIOLATED OR IF I AM A VICTIM OF DISCRIMINATION?

If you think one of your constitutional rights has been violated, you can call the Center for Constitutional Rights at (212) 614-6464, or a similar group in your area (such as the American Civil Liberties Union) which is operated for the purpose of advocating and defending people's civil rights. As noted before, if you believe you are a victim of job discrimination, you can call the federal Equal Employment Opportunity Commission. If you feel you are a victim of discrimination in housing, you can call your local office of the federal Department of Housing and Urban Development for assistance. Or you can locate an attorney specializing in constitutional law or discrimination law (see the first section on choosing an attorney).

HOW LONG DO I HAVE TO FILE A CIVIL-RIGHTS VIOLATION CLAIM OR A DISCRIMINATION CLAIM?

The amount of time you have to act varies with the type of claim you are making. For instance, if you're filing a complaint of discrimination in employment by reason of race, color, sex, religion, or national origin, you may have 180 days from the date of the act you are complaining of to file with the Equal Employment Opportunity Commission. (Under state law, you may have more time, depending on where you live.) If you have a claim that you were discriminated against in housing by reason of race, color, sex, religion, national origin, handicap, or familial status, you have 365 days to make a written claim to your local office (or the Washington, D.C., office) of the federal Department of Housing and Urban Development. As in any legal matter, it is wise to act promptly so your rights under the law are not cut off simply because you did not file a complaint on time.

CAN A "PRIVATE" CLUB EXCLUDE ME FROM MEMBERSHIP BECAUSE OF MY COLOR?

A club that is truly private—that is, does not admit nonmembers for any purpose—can lawfully refuse to admit you for any reason the members choose. However, if a "private" club also allows nonmembers to hire catered affairs on the club property, it may be considered to be a public place—and a public place can't discriminate because of race, color, religion, sex, or national origin.

CAN AN EMPLOYER DISCRIMINATE AGAINST ME BECAUSE I AM HANDICAPPED?

Under federal law effective July 26, 1992, an employer with twenty-five or more employees can't discriminate against you because you are handicapped. That is, if you and another, non-handicapped person are equally qualified for the job, the employer can't use your handicap to disqualify you from the position. In 1994, all employers who have fifteen or more employees will fall under the coverage of this law. However, an employer with only nine employees is exempt from the provisions of these laws and can lawfully exclude you from a job because you are handicapped. There may be state or local laws that protect handicapped persons from job discrimination. If you feel you are the victim of job discrimination because you are handicapped, get advice from a local attorney.

I FILED A DISCRIMINATION COMPLAINT AGAINST MY EMPLOYER AND MY EMPLOYER IS NOW HARASSING ME. IS THAT LEGAL?

No, it is not. Your employer can be punished for both the original act of discrimination and the later harassment for filing the complaint. If your employer denied you a promotion because of your race and then failed to give you a pay raise because you filed the discrimination complaint, your employer can be punished for both acts.

WHEN I STARTED PASSING OUT PAMPHLETS IN THE STREET ADVERTISING MY NEW BUSINESS, A POLICE OFFICER ORDERED ME TO STOP AND SAID I WAS VIOLATING THE LAW. ISN'T MY RIGHT TO FREE SPEECH PROTECTED?

It depends. If your new business was a brothel, and there was a local law prohibiting the advertising of prostitution, you would be in violation of the law. (States have the right to restrict advertising of services or products that may be harmful to the health, safety, or welfare of its citizens.)

However, if you had opened up a new supermarket and were advertising its grand opening, you couldn't legally be barred from distributing your advertising in a public place. (A local law might properly require you to clean up the mess from discarded pamphlets after you were finished.)

But if you want to hand out your supermarket pamphlets inside a privately owned shopping mall, you'll have to get permission from the owner of the mall first, since owners of private property can legally prohibit distribution of advertising materials on their property.

CAN THE GOVERNMENT RESTRICT MY FREEDOM OF SPEECH IF I AM PART OF A PROTEST?

Yes. Although freedom of speech is guaranteed by the United States Constitution, the federal or state government may restrict your right to protest under certain circumstances. If in your protest you commit violence or create a "clear and present danger" that violence will erupt, the police can arrest you to keep the peace. If you obstruct traffic while demonstrating, the police have a right to restrict your protest to the sidewalk so normal traffic flow can proceed. If you are making an extreme amount of noise while protesting (such as shouting in a hospital zone), the police can instruct you to cease the extreme noise and protest more quietly. If you are picketing for an unlawful purpose (such as protesting as a cover-up for a bank robbery), your right to free speech can be curtailed. Or, if you are protesting for the purpose of intimidating a judge or a jury in court, this type of "speech" is not protected under the law.

CAN A LANDLORD REFUSE TO HAVE ME AS A TENANT BECAUSE I AM A SINGLE MOTHER?

If the property has five or more rental units, the landlord cannot legally exclude you because you are a single mother, since that would be discrimination based upon familial status, which is prohibited by federal law. Federal law also prohibits discrimination in housing based upon race, color, religion, sex or national origin, or handicap.

Your state or local law may have additional categories of persons who cannot be denied housing.

If the property had less than five living units, however, it would be exempt from compliance with this law and you could legally be refused housing. Once again, check your state and local laws for housing regulations.

CAN A DOCTOR REFUSE TO TREAT ME BECAUSE I HAVE ACQUIRED IMMUNE DEFICIENCY SYNDROME (AIDS)?

When doctors choose the profession of medicine, they take an oath that they will render care to persons in need. If a doctor refuses to treat you, you can lodge a complaint with your local medical association.

However, unless a law has been passed in your area that requires doctors to treat AIDS patients, doctors are legally free, as private citizens, to render or refuse to render medical treatment to any person for any reason. But if a doctor started to treat you and later found out you had AIDS and wanted to terminate her relationship with you, she may have a legal duty to turn over your care to someone of equal or better training. She could not turn your care over to a nurse, for instance; she must turn over your care to a physician.

MY LOCAL NEWSPAPER PRINTED AN ARTICLE CONTAINING FALSE INFORMATION ABOUT ME. CAN I SUE THEM FOR LIBEL?

You can sue for libel, but whether you'd win or not is a different story.

If you are a public official (such as the mayor or the police chief), you would have to prove both that the information was false and that the newspaper acted "with malice"—knowing that the information was false or printed without regard to its truth. The same would apply if you are a "public figure," such as the owner of a large corporation, or someone who has been thrust into the public eye (say you just won a $10 million lottery or saved a small boy from a burning building).

If you are a private citizen without any special notoriety, you would only have to prove that the article contained false and damaging information about you and that the newspaper was negligent in printing this information.

DOES ANYONE HAVE THE RIGHT TO RECORD MY TELEPHONE CONVERSATIONS?

In most states, it is illegal to tape record phone conversations in which you are not involved. In other words, you can't "bug" someone else's telephone and record his conversations without his permission. If you are one of the parties using the telephone, however, you can record the conversation, even if you don't tell the person on the other end.

There are times when you may be asked for permission to tape your conversation, for instance, if you are making an insurance claim over the telephone, the insurance company may ask you for permission to record the conversation. You may be deemed to consent to the recording of your conversations if you call "911" for police, ambulance, fire, or other emergency assistance. Such conversations are routinely recorded in the public interest so that the tape can be replayed if the "911" caller spoke too quickly before hanging up and the "911" operator could not write down all of the information necessary to send out help.

A court order may also be issued to allow the police to record your telephone conversations under certain circumstances, such as if you are suspected of committing crimes like murder, kidnapping, robbery, extortion, espionage, sabotage, treason, or rioting.

I WANT TO BUY A HANDGUN BUT THE GUN DEALER TOLD ME THAT I MUST GET A LICENSE FIRST. DOESN'T THE CONSTITUTION GUARANTEE ME THE RIGHT TO "BEAR ARMS"?

No. The Second Amendment to the Constitution was intended to protect local and state militias from interference from the federal government in the early days of this country. This amendment does not guarantee that each citizen has the right to own or use a firearm. Federal and state governments have the right to restrict the sale and ownership of guns, so long as the restrictions are reasonable. For example, your state can require that you be at least eighteen years of age and have no record of criminal convictions in order to purchase a firearm legally. Also, your local laws can require that all handguns be concealed from sight when being carried from place to place (as opposed to the Old West, when you wore your holster and "six-gun" in plain sight). Consult your local laws to determine what requirements you must meet to acquire the right to possess or use a gun.

ARE GOVERNMENT DOCUMENTS AVAILABLE TO ME FOR COPYING AND INSPECTION?

Sometimes. Under the federal Freedom of Information Act, the public may be entitled to inspect and copy certain government books and records. The government can withhold certain information, such as information necessary for national or foreign security, internal personnel records, income tax returns, and confidential commercial or financial information obtained from a private citizen.

The government must tell you within ten business days whether they will honor your request and must determine an appeal or a denial of your request within twenty business days. The government is entitled to time to gather the information you requested, so you will not necessarily gain immediate access to the documents after your request has been approved.

SECTION 9

GOING FOR BROKE: SMART QUESTIONS TO ASK ABOUT BANKRUPTCY AND CREDITORS' RIGHTS

You've worked hard all your life. It's been a struggle, but you've managed to make a decent living for you and your family. Suddenly you become very ill—and your life savings slip away in doctors' bills, hospital costs, and the basic costs of living while you're unable to work.

Your health is rapidly improving, but your financial situation is not. What can you do? Before you do anything, ask questions. Find out what options are open to you. Be sure that you understand what your rights are, and what your responsibilities are. What would you lose if you declared bankruptcy? What would you gain?

The bankruptcy system was set up to help people in times of great need. But it can be a difficult, and emotionally trying process. You'll need careful planning and good advice. This is no time to sit back and let someone else make your decisions for you. You need to find out every-thing you can about how bankruptcy works, and how it can work for you.

SHOULD I FILE FOR BANKRUPTCY?

If extraordinary medical bills, business setbacks, or other situations have brought the creditors to your doorstep, you may be a good candidate for filing a peti-tion for bankruptcy relief.

Nobody wants to file for bankruptcy. But there are times when circumstances make it impossible to fulfill heavy financial obligations. Bankruptcy relief laws were enacted to help people who get into debt to "wipe the slate clean" and get a new start on life without the specter of past debt over their shoulders.

What if you suffered a heart attack while between jobs, and you had no medical insurance coverage? You amassed significant hospital bills, doctors' bills, and medical proce-dure fees. You've been trying to pay each of your creditors a bit at a time to try to keep them happy, but you owe them all money. Even though you're now back on the job, your creditors are hounding you for payment. Several of your creditors have brought lawsuits against you for the outstanding money. In the middle of this nightmare, you find out that your checking account has been "frozen": one of your creditors has a judgment against you, and had a restraining order issued against your bank account, so you can't use that bank account to pay anyone else.

In this case, filing a bankruptcy petition may be the only reasonable alternative for you to pursue.

WHAT TYPES OF BANKRUPTCY COURT HEARINGS MUST I APPEAR AT IF I FILE A BANKRUPTCY PETITION?

Bankruptcy laws were enacted to help you get out of debt in the worst of times—they were not designed to make it quick or easy. There are several court appearances you must make if you file for bankruptcy.

At your first required court appearance, the bankruptcy court and/or your creditors will have the right to question you regarding your assets and liabilities. If your bank account shows a withdrawal of $10,000 one month before you filed the bankruptcy petition, you should be prepared to explain why you withdrew the money and to whom it was paid. (If it was given to someone to pay an old debt, or as a gift, or as an attempt to hide your assets in anticipation of the bankruptcy proceeding, the court may have a right to reclaim the money from the person whom you paid.)

If a claim of one or more of your creditors is disputed, or if someone questions your prebankruptcy transfers of money or assets, you may be required to make additional court appearances. For instance, if you listed your debt as $10,000, but the bank claims it's $20,000, you may have to resolve the discrepancy in a bankruptcy court hearing.

You'll also be required to attend a final hearing as to whether your debts should be forgiven ("discharged"). At that time, anyone who has reason to believe that you should not be discharged from your debts has the right to make an objection and be heard. If you transferred your $40,000 automobile to your mother as a "gift" a week before you filed your bankruptcy petition, your other creditors will probably object to your discharge on the basis that you made a fraudulent transfer with the intent to hinder, delay, or defraud your creditors. Your attorney should accompany you to these hearings and fully explain their nature and purpose.

WILL FILING A BANKRUPTCY PETITION STOP MY CREDITORS FROM HOUNDING ME FOR MONEY?

As soon as you file your bankruptcy petition, an automatic "stay" goes into effect, stopping most creditors from pursuing their claims against you.

Say you still owe the hospital money following your heart attack. Its accounting office has been calling you and sending you letters demanding payment of your bill. Once you've filed your bankruptcy petition, it must stop all collection efforts. What if your car loan payments are also delinquent and your bank has been threatening to repossess? Once you've filed your petition, it can neither take your car nor request money from you unless it gets specific permission from the bankruptcy court.

All creditors must stop collection efforts unless they get a special order from the bankruptcy court, or they're exempt from (not subject to the rules of) the automatic stay.

WILL I HAVE TO PAY ANY OF MY DEBTS?

A bankruptcy proceeding will not stop collection of alimony, maintenance, or support from assets that are exempt from inclusion in the bankrupt's "estate" (assets that can be used to pay off creditors), such as the family automobile. Similarly, the filing of a bankruptcy petition will not stop a criminal proceeding against you, nor will it stop an action by the government to enforce its police power, as these actions are exempt from the automatic stay.

WILL THE REST OF MY DEBTS BE FORGIVEN IF I FILE A BANKRUPTCY PETITION?

Each debt will be considered separately, and whether or not it will be forgiven depends on the type of debt involved and the circumstances relating to it. Depending upon the type of debt you have, you may have to repay all or only a part of a particular debt. Certain creditors may have to be paid in full, including lenders whose loans are secured by assets (such as a mortgage on your home or a car loan).

Other creditors, such as credit card companies, may not have to be paid in full by you. Ask your lawyer to go over your list of creditors with you to determine which debts can be discharged and which cannot.

WHAT ARE SOME OF THE FACTORS THAT DETERMINE WHICH DEBTS ARE FORGIVEN AND WHICH ARE NOT?

First, all debts you want to have discharged must be listed by you in your bankruptcy petition. If you don't list a creditor, and he doesn't file a notice of claim to bring himself into the bankruptcy proceeding, that debt will not be discharged. You'll have to pay him what you owe, and he can continue to hound you for the money after the bankruptcy is over.

Secondly, only debts that existed prior to the date of the filing of your petition can be discharged in the bankruptcy proceeding. If you go out the day after you file the petition and incur a new debt by purchasing a television set with your credit card, that new purchase will not be discharged in the bankruptcy proceeding.

Thirdly, some debts are not dischargeable under the law. As stated earlier, alimony, maintenance, and child support obligations are not dischargeable, nor are certain taxes or certain student loans. Also, if discharge of a debt was denied in a previous bankruptcy, you cannot now try to get it discharged.

Fourthly, a specific objection can be made to deny discharge to a particular debt that is otherwise dischargeable. This category includes debts incurred by fraud or debts resulting from a willful and malicious injury (such as damages you have to pay from a lawsuit brought by someone whose nose you broke without provocation in a barroom brawl).

And, finally, if you have failed to act properly or failed to cooperate with the bankruptcy court, a discharge of all of your debts may be denied.

WHAT IS MEANT BY "FAILURE TO ACT PROPERLY" OR "FAILURE TO COOPERATE WITH THE BANKRUPTCY COURT"?

You must prove to the court that you are filing for bankruptcy in good faith and with good reason. Some of the grounds for denial of a discharge of all of your debts are as follows:

1. You knowingly concealed assets, such as accumulating a large amount of cash and not declaring it as one of your assets in your petition;
2. You failed to keep books and records or knowingly concealed them from the court;
3. You knowingly and fraudulently lied in your bankruptcy petition or under oath, such as knowingly undervaluing your assets when reporting them to the bankruptcy court;
4. You were unable to explain a loss of assets (such as the $10,000 withdrawal from your bank account);
5. You failed to obey a court order directing you to answer questions about your financial status by invoking the Fifth Amendment; or
6. You had filed a bankruptcy petition within the last six years (unless you have a payout-style bankruptcy where you make periodic payments into court to pay your debts, in which case you may file even if it hasn't been six years since your last petition).

ARE THERE DIFFERENT TYPES OF BANKRUPTCY?

There are basically two types of bankruptcy proceedings: a "straight" liquidation-type proceeding and a payout-style proceeding.

If you file a straight liquidation-type bankruptcy, you must turn over all nonexempt assets into the bankruptcy court. Your assets will be sold, and the proceeds distributed to your creditors.

If you file a payout-style of bankruptcy proceeding and it is approved by the court, you and the court will arrange a payout over time of all or a portion of past-due debts. So long as you live up to the payment schedule, you will generally be permitted to keep your assets.

However, you must show the court that by arranging for such a payment schedule, your creditors will be at least as well off as if all of your assets were "liquidated" (sold) in a "straight" bankruptcy proceeding. If you own assets worth $150,000 and you owe debts of $100,000, you must propose in your bankruptcy payout plan to pay your creditors at least the $100,000 they would have gotten if you had turned in all of your assets, sold them, and divided the proceeds. Otherwise, your creditors will be able to petition the court to convert your payout-style bankruptcy proceeding to a "straight" proceeding in which your assets will be sold.

HOW DO I KNOW WHICH TYPE OF BANKRUPTCY PROCEEDING TO CHOOSE?

If you have large debts and few assets, a "straight" liquidation-style bankruptcy may be a good choice, since you will only lose the few assets you have. So, if you have high medical bills but live in an apartment and own only your clothes, a television set, and some personal items, a "straight" bankruptcy may be good for you.

However, if you have assets you wish to protect, a pay-out-style may be a better way for you to go. If you own a home, or have assets such as antique jewelry or rare books that you want to keep, and you have a regular income from which you can make periodic payments into the court, a payout-style proceeding may be the right choice for you.

WHICH OF MY ASSETS WILL BE INCLUDED IN MY BANKRUPTCY "ESTATE" AND WHICH ONES WILL BE EXEMPT?

All of your assets will be included in your bankruptcy estate unless they are specifically exempt by state or federal law. The federal law has one set of exemptions, but gives the option to the individual states to substitute their own set of exemptions, if they wish.

For instance, your state may provide that your exempt property includes such items as a motor vehicle not exceeding a certain value, social security payments, alimony, or unemployment benefits, one stove, one sewing machine, the family Bible, domestic animals, clothing, household furniture, a wedding ring, a "homestead" exemption of a certain dollar amount above liens and encumbrances on your residence, and a burial plot.

WHAT IS A HOMESTEAD EXEMPTION?

A homestead exemption is a sum of money (for instance $10,000) over and above the mortgages and encumbrances on your home, which you are allowed to keep if your home must be sold to pay off your debts.

Suppose you owned a house worth $125,000, and your mortgage and other encumbrances totaled $120,000.

Assuming the house was sold at its fair market to pay off your debts, your creditors would get $115,000 and you would receive the homestead exemption of $10,000. If you and your wife jointly own the house, the creditors would get $105,000, and you and your wife would get $20,000 ($10,000 for each of you).

WILL I LOSE MY HOME IF I FILE FOR BANKRUPTCY?

Depending upon the type of bankruptcy petition you and your attorney choose to file and the equity value of your home (that is, the fair market value of your home, less mortgages and other liens), you may be able to keep your home or business after you file a bankruptcy petition.

If you file a liquidation-type bankruptcy proceeding, you must turn over all of your nonexempt assets into the bankruptcy court; they will be sold, and the proceeds distributed to your creditors. If your home is worth $125,000 and mortgages and other liens total $100,000, your equity value is $25,000. If your applicable homestead exemption is $10,000, you will have to turn your home over to the bankruptcy court for sale, since there is $15,000 value in your home over and above your homestead exemption.

However, if the equity value of your home does not exceed the homestead exemption, you will be able to keep your home. So, if you owned that same home worth $125,000 and you had mortgages and liens of $115,000, you would be able to keep your home because your equity value ($10,000) equals your homestead exemption ($10,000).

In a payout-type bankruptcy, you will keep your home and pay your mortgage as part of your monthly installment payments into the bankruptcy court. If your mortgage is in arrears, you must, over the term of your installment payments, bring your mortgage up to date as well as keep up your current payments. Whether or not you will be able to keep your home is a factor you and your attorney must consider in selecting the type of bankruptcy that is best for you.

WILL ALL OF MY UNSECURED CREDITORS BE PAID THE SAME PERCENTAGE OF THEIR DEBTS, OR WILL CERTAIN CLASSES OF CREDITORS BE PAID FIRST AND OTHERS BE LEFT WITH LESS?

The bankruptcy laws provide certain priorities of expenses and claims. Before any unsecured debts are paid, administrative expenses, such as payment of attorneys' fees, bankruptcy court filing fees, and auctioneers' fees are paid first. (This may seem like an unfair system, and in essence, it is—unless you are the attorney handling the case. But this is, however, the way the law now stands.) Then, other types of payments are paid in a certain order.

Wages and salaries of employees receive a high priority, as well as contributions to an employee benefit plan. Certain taxes, such as income tax and property tax, also receive a high priority, but only after wages, salaries, and employee benefit contributions. Other taxes (such as customs taxes or excise taxes) receive a priority, but only after most other types of taxes.

If, after paying all of these priority items, there is nothing left for the other creditors, they are basically out of luck.

WILL OTHERS BE ABLE TO DENY ME CREDIT IF I FILE FOR BANKRUPTCY?

Yes, they can. There's no federal law prohibiting a creditor from denying you new credit once you've filed a bankruptcy petition. Unfortunately, once you've gotten yourself into an unfavorable financial situation, future creditors have good reason to be skeptical about your ability to pay your bills.

If you're asked on a credit application whether or not you've ever filed for bankruptcy, you must answer honestly. If you perjure yourself by lying, you'll be in more hot water than ever. If you're caught lying, you face the possibility of criminal charges.

WILL FILING A BANKRUPTCY PETITION STOP LAWSUITS THAT ARE CURRENTLY PENDING AGAINST ME?

Filing of a petition in bankruptcy will automatically stop all civil (non-criminal) lawsuits against you, including an action to foreclose a mortgage on your home. Let's go back to the hospital again: if the hospital is currently suing you for the past-due bills, it must stop the lawsuit and take no further action except in the bankruptcy court.

If your creditor has a good reason for continuing his or her lawsuit, however, he or she may apply to the bankruptcy court to allow the lawsuit to continue. For instance, if your spouse is suing you for past-due alimony payments (alimony payments are not dischargeable) and is seeking to collect from otherwise exempt assets (such as the family car or your social security payments), she may apply to have the automatic stay lifted so she can continue her lawsuit against you.

WHAT IF A CREDITOR ALREADY HAS COMPLETED HIS LAWSUIT AND NOW HAS A JUDGMENT AGAINST ME FOR THE MONEY OWED. WILL A BANKRUPTCY PETITION CANCEL THIS DEBT?

After a bankruptcy petition has been filed by you, a judgment creditor (that is, a creditor who has a judgment against you obtained in a prior lawsuit) must stop all enforcement proceedings (such as sending the sheriff to visit you or your bank) to try to collect the debt.

The bankruptcy proceeding may determine that you pay this creditor a certain portion of the judgment due. After you've paid this amount, the court will issue an order discharging you of the obligation of paying this debt. That means that the creditor will no longer be able to collect the rest of his money unless you also own real estate and the judgment has been filed as a lien against your real estate more than 120 days before you filed your bankruptcy petition.

This is confusing to many people, including attorneys, who think that all judgments are automatically forgiven in full after you file your bankruptcy petition. If you own real estate, however, it may be a different story.

WHAT HAPPENS IF MY HUSBAND FILES A PETITION IN BANKRUPTCY AND I DON'T? WHAT WILL HAPPEN TO OUR JOINTLY HELD ASSETS?

If your spouse files a petition in bankruptcy and you don't, you will have to prove how much of your jointly owned assets are "owned" by you, by showing how much you contributed to that asset. If both you and your spouse always worked, and received equal salaries, you would have a good case for proving that one half of the jointly held assets really belong to you. If you cannot prove a contribution, the law says that the entire asset may be deemed to be an asset of his bankruptcy estate.

If you own a house jointly with your husband and he files a bankruptcy petition and you don't, the bankruptcy court technically may have the right to sell your interest in the house. However, this is not often done, since courts are reluctant to throw a spouse out of her own home, and may not be permitted to do so in some states.

BEFORE FILING HIS BANKRUPTCY PETITION, MY FATHER GAVE GIFTS TO ME AND MY SISTERS. DO WE NOW HAVE TO GIVE THE GIFTS BACK?

Perhaps. If the gift was made more than one year before the filing of the bankruptcy petition, you do not have to turn it over to the bankruptcy court. If, however, the gift was made within one year of the filing of the bankruptcy petition, you may have to turn over the value of the gift to the bankruptcy court.

The same rule applies in cases where you may have paid less than full value for an asset transferred to you by someone who later files a bankruptcy petition. If your father transfers his $80,000 waterfront home to you for $20,000 within one year of filing his bankruptcy petition, you may be the recipient of a "fraudulent" transfer, and you'll have to account to the bankruptcy court for the $60,000 difference between the market value of the property and the purchase price you paid for it. (If you don't have the money, you may have to declare bankruptcy yourself.) If the same transfer was made a year and a day before you file the petition, you can keep the home with no questions asked.

IF SOMEONE OWES ME MONEY AND FILES A BANKRUPTCY PETITION, WHAT ARE MY RIGHTS?

Do not assume that all is lost if someone who owes you money files a petition for bankruptcy! You have the right to file your own proof of claim if the debtor fails to list your debt or lists your debt incorrectly in the bankruptcy petition.

You have the right to examine the debtor concerning her assets and liabilities, to determine whether the debtor may have assets she is hiding or that she transferred to someone as a preferential transfer.

Depending upon the type of debt and the type of bankruptcy petition filed, you may be repaid either in part or in full, either in a lump sum or over a period of time. You may be eligible to apply for a court order allowing you to continue a lawsuit or to commence a lawsuit against the debtor if you believe your rights have been prejudiced by some act of the debtor. You may be able to prevent your particular debt from being discharged, or you may be able to block a discharge of the debt completely, for the reasons discussed under previous questions.

SOMEONE WHO OWES ME MONEY IS PAYING SOME OF HIS CREDITORS BUT NOT ME. WHAT CAN I DO?

You may be able to file a bankruptcy petition against a debtor and force the debtor to pay you equitably with others.

To file an involuntary petition in bankruptcy, you must be owed at least $5,000. If the debtor has less than twelve creditors, you may file the petition on your own; otherwise, you need others to join you in filing the bankruptcy petition against the debtor.

In essence, you are forcing this person into bankruptcy. You may prefer this option over simply bringing a lawsuit against him for this reason: Suppose you suspect he has hidden assets. The bankruptcy court will find these assets and force equal payment at little or no expense to you. The bankruptcy court does all that work. If you sued, you'd have to pay your attorney to find these assets.

However, if it turns out that your suspicions were unfounded, the debtor may be able to sue you for damages, including costs of getting the bankruptcy petition dismissed, reasonable attorneys' fees, and punitive (punishment) damages for filing a frivolous petition. So you should do some investigative work before you take the action of filing an involuntary petition against a debtor of yours.

I GOT A SUMMONS FROM THE BANKRUPTCY COURT REQUESTING THAT I RETURN MONEY PAID TO ME BY SOMEONE WHO HAS NOW FILED A PETITION IN BANKRUPTCY. DO I HAVE TO GIVE THE MONEY BACK?

Depending upon the nature of the debt, the date of the payment, and your relationship to the debtor, you may or may not have to return the money to the bankruptcy court.

Say you had loaned the debtor money to buy a new car, and the debtor pledged his car to you as security for the loan. If the debtor paid you in full five days before he filed his bankruptcy petition, you would not have to pay any of the money back, since you would be entitled to full payment under the bankruptcy proceeding as a secured creditor.

If, however, you loaned your brother $5,000 as an "unsecured" loan (that is, with no asset pledged as security) and he paid you in full within one year of filing his bankruptcy petition, you may have to return the money to the bankruptcy court. As a relative you would be considered an "insider" and if you were paid more than you would have been entitled to get in the bankruptcy proceeding for a debt in your same category, you will have to give it back. If, however, he had repaid his loan to you a year and one day before filing the petition, you would not have to return the money.

IF MY BUSINESS GOES BANKRUPT, AM I PERSONALLY LIABLE?

Not necessarily. It is the same concept as starting your own business and becoming a corporation. That way you guarantee that you are not personally liable for any moneys due—the corporation is liable.

It's the same with bankruptcy. If you declare your business to be bankrupt, your personal assets are still yours to keep. However, if you have any personal guarantees on business debts, those would be affected. Suppose you take out a loan in order to buy a $100,000 printing machine for your business, and put up your house as collateral on the loan. If your business then goes bankrupt, your house would be considered as part of the business assets (and it's possible you could lose your home).

If you have no such personal guarantees, business and personal bankruptcy are two totally separate areas.

SECTION 10

THE GRIM REAPER: SMART QUESTIONS TO ASK ABOUT WILLS AND ESTATES

Nobody likes to think about dying. A lot of us put off dealing with issues of wills and estates because of the superstitious feeling that this somehow brings death nearer. However, no one I know has ever died from making out a will.

There's no way of knowing what will happen tomorrow. Dealing with these issues today will probably bring you peace of mind, knowing your affairs have been put in order.

A will can be very simple, or it can be a complicated, multilayered document. It depends on your financial status and how you plan to distribute your assets after you're gone. There's no way that we could have included questions here to cover your personal situation. But we've tried to include the most general and universal questions and examples so that you can use them for a basis of comparison.

Read these questions (and answers) carefully before you speak to your lawyer. Choose the ones that are most relevant to you. Write down what your lawyer says, and compare his answers with the ones in the book. If there are things you still don't understand, ask your lawyer to clarify and explain further. Use the questions in this section, plus any others you can think of, to get information related specifically to you and your personal circumstances.

DO I REALLY NEED A WILL?

There's one thing you know for sure: "You can't take it with you." So if you're concerned about who'll get your money and possessions after you die, then you should have a will. If you don't, the laws of your state will dictate where your money goes, regardless of your wishes.

Suppose you have a brother you've hated all your life, and you swore he'd never see one red cent of your money. If you're a single person and both of your parents are deceased, and you have no will, the state could mandate that your assets be divided equally among all your brothers and sisters—whether you liked them or not.

If you're married, but have no children and no will, your state may dictate that your parents inherit a share of your property; you may wish, however, to have your spouse of twenty years inherit everything.

If you do have children, the state may assign a portion of your estate to them. You may (wisely so) wish to give all of your money to your spouse instead, knowing that he'll take good care of the entire family in your absence and be less likely to squander your money.

Leaving no will means that your estate will be divided according to the law and the law alone. Your personal feelings and intentions won't be taken into account. So if you care about who gets what or want to make sure your wishes are carried out, you'd better have a will.

WHO INHERITS MY PROPERTY IF I DON'T HAVE A WILL?

Many people think that if you don't leave a will, "the state" will inherit your money. This is not so—unless no other relatives specified in the law can be found.

Normally, your spouse, your children, and/or your parents (if any) are the first in line under states' laws to inherit your estate. If you have no spouse, children, or parents, then your brothers and sisters, aunts and uncles, nephews and nieces, cousins, and/or grandparents may be eligible to claim a portion of your estate.

Each state has specific laws governing who will inherit your property. For instance, if you have a spouse and two children and die without a will, the laws of your state will have a formula, such as one-third to the spouse and two-thirds to the children, which will be applied in dividing up your property.

If you're married but have no children, your spouse and possibly your parents may be entitled to your property. If you're unmarried and have no surviving parents, your brothers and sisters may inherit from you if you die. In essence, if you don't have your own will, the state will create one for you upon your death.

HOW OLD DO I HAVE TO BE TO MAKE OUT A WILL?

The age at which you can legally make out a will usually corresponds to the "age of majority" of your state, that is, the age at which that state considers you to be an adult. In some states, it may be age eighteen; in other states, it may be age twenty-one.

Before you reach that age, your state considers that you lack the maturity to properly make the choices called for in a will. Even if you are a very mature person, but you are under the age for a will in your state, you cannot legally make out a will.

WHEN DO I NEED A LAWYER TO DRAW UP A WILL?

Wills need not be complicated documents. There are now many commercially prepared forms you can simply buy and fill out on your own. But there are special circumstances when a lawyer is advised or required, such as when:

- there are several complex matters involved. If you have any questions, it's best to consult a lawyer;
- your estate is large enough that you should be concerned about reducing death taxes;
- you own a business. Will the business shut down if you die? Can it be sold, or kept running? It usually takes a lawyer's expertise to make proper plans for business;
- you want to disinherit a spouse or a child. If there's any chance your will might be challenged, a lawyer should draw it up.

IS THERE ANY WAY I CAN AVOID HAVING A WILL?

There are no real advantages in avoiding having a will (except possibly the cost of the will itself and any court fees that may be due to probate the will). However, if all of your assets are set up in such a way that they automatically go to a designated beneficiary (like a bank account in trust for your brother), and you have no children for whom you should appoint a guardian and no other special interests to protect (such as a mentally disabled adult child for whom you wish to place money in trust), you may be able to avoid having a will and still have your estate distributed to the persons you designate.

Say you own a house in joint names with your brother with a right of survivorship (if one dies, the other one gets ownership) specified in the deed. Upon your death, the entire house will go to your brother. Similarly, if you have a bank account with your nephew with a right of survivorship, the money in the account will go to him upon your death. Your bank account is "in trust for" your daughter, and upon your death the money in the account will pass to her. Your life insurance policy and pension plan are payable directly to your husband. You have divided your assets among your family without a will.

If you choose to concoct your own scheme to avoid having a will, however, you may encounter some unanticipated pitfalls. If you decide to cut off your spouse, your spouse may have a right under your state's law to claim a portion of assets you gave to others.

If you give disproportionate shares to your four children (for instance, you took $10,000 from your oldest son's joint account just before you died), he may go to court after you die to try to claim the rest of his "share." To avoid possible family squabbling after you die, it would probably be easier in the long run to have an attorney draw up a will to make your intentions clearly known and less subject to attack.

MY ATTORNEY AGREED TO SUPERVISE THE SIGNING OF MY WILL, BUT TOLD ME THAT I NEEDED AT LEAST TWO WITNESSES. WHO WOULD BE A VALID WITNESS?

When you execute your will, you want it to be witnessed by people who are not related to you by blood or marriage and who are not named in the will, either as a beneficiary (someone who inherits something from you) or a fiduciary (someone who is to act as an administrator or executor of your will). Neighbors or friends would be a good choice if they're not your relatives or beneficiaries under your will.

You want a disinterested witness in the event one of your relatives or one of your beneficiaries is unhappy with the provisions of your will. Let's say you cut your daughter out of your will because she left home when she was eighteen, married a man you hated, and hasn't contacted you in twenty years. When your estate is administered in court, she'll receive legal notice of your death. Then she may suddenly show up, claiming a portion of your estate.

What if one of your witnesses was your cousin/beneficiary and the other one was your executor under the will? Your daughter may claim that their swearing to your "testamentary capacity" (your mental capacity to make a will) was tainted by their interest in the will. She may try to convince the court that you were actually a raving lunatic who cut her out of the will for no reason. She could ask that the will be set aside and your estate distributed under the law as if there was no will (in which case your daughter would receive a share). If successful, your daughter may get the money you worked so hard to keep away from her—just because you chose the wrong witnesses.

CAN I CHANGE MY WILL WHENEVER I WANT AND AS MANY TIMES AS I WANT?

Yes. However, you can't take a pen and make your own changes to your existing will without creating trouble. If you alter a will once it has been executed, and then you die, your heirs will have a field day fighting over what you really intended to do.

Suppose you have a bequest in your will that leaves $10,000 to your favorite nephew. Your nephew forgets to send you a birthday card, and you decide to cut him out of your will. You cross out his name and substitute your niece's. After you die, your niece and nephew will probably have a long battle in court over who should really get the money.

What if you decide your entire will is bad and rip it up in shreds without executing another will? After your death, your heirs find a copy you forgot to destroy. Those heirs who would have inherited under the will claim the original was lost and seek to have the copy admitted to court. However, the rest of your family wants to prove that you purposely destroyed the original, since they would stand to inherit if there was no will. You have succeeded in creating turmoil and mystery, and the court—not you—will determine who gets your inheritance.

WHAT'S THE BEST WAY TO PROTECT MY WILL AGAINST CHANGES AFTER I DIE?

Your attorney can place your will in her safe-deposit box or file it with the court after you sign it, and it can stay there until you die. If your will is in either of these safe places, none of your friends or relatives will have access to it, so they will not be able to alter or destroy your will either before or after you die.

Never place your will in your own safe-deposit box. After you die, your own safe-deposit box may become sealed by law and a court order may be required to open it up; meanwhile, your beneficiaries cannot offer your will for probate. (And until your will is probated, no one may have access to your assets for either living expenses or for paying your bills.)

WHAT IS PROBATE?

Probate is the process by which a will is proven to be valid. A written petition is presented to the court with the original copy of the will. All of the persons who inherit under the will, as well as all of the persons who would inherit if there were no will, must receive formal written notice of the intended probate of the will. All challenges as to the validity of the will must also be presented to the court. After all challenges are considered, the court will determine whether the will should be declared as valid.

MY GREAT-UNCLE HAS THREE WILLS, ALL EXECUTED WITHIN TWO MONTHS OF EACH OTHER. THE LATEST ONE LISTS ME AS BENEFICIARY. HOW DO I PROVE WHICH WILL IS VALID?

Your family could be in for a long court battle. Each of the wills will be reviewed by the court to try to sort out just what your great-uncle had in mind when he executed these wills. The latest one may not necessarily be the one declared valid.

If you want to prove that a will is valid, you have to present a petition to the court. The will must have been legally executed, including having the proper number of witnesses and being in the proper form. The witnesses may be required to come to court to testify that the will was properly executed and that the deceased had sufficient mental presence and knowledge of the objects of his bounty. If there are several conflicting wills, the court will examine all the wills to determine which one, if any, should be declared as the valid will.

I HAVE BEEN LEFT MONEY IN A DECEASED RELATIVE'S WILL. ANOTHER RELATIVE, WHO WAS CUT OUT OF THE WILL, IS UNHAPPY. CAN THE EXCLUDED RELATIVE CHALLENGE THE WILL?

There are two factors that come into play in a case like this:

1. The relationship to the deceased. Is the excluded relative a spouse, a child, or only a distant relative?
2. The circumstances surrounding the execution of the will. Did someone "poison" the mind of the deceased to exclude the other relative?

If you want to "get even" with your spouse by cutting him out of your will, for instance, your efforts may be foiled by laws that protect the right of a spouse to inherit. Many states have laws that provide that the excluded spouse may claim a portion of the estate. In this case, the relationship of the spouse is the deciding factor.

Circumstances may be more important if you decide to cut one of your children out of the will. Suppose you have three children, and you purposely omit child number three from your testamentary scheme (your will). That child may be out of luck.

Suppose, however, you have a will that was written when you only had two children. The will specifically mentions child number one and child number two by name. Then you have child number three and forget to update your will. Child number three may be able to prove that you inadvertently left her out and successfully claim a portion of your estate.

Or, if children number one and two told you lies about child number three (how she only wanted your money and didn't care about you at all), which influenced you to purposely exclude her from your will, child number three may be able to prove that her siblings poisoned your mind and successfully claim a proportionate share of the inheritance.

ARE WILLS DRAWN UP IN ANOTHER STATE (OR COUNTRY) VALID?

Yes, if your will was validly executed according to the laws of the other state or country. Let's say the state where you currently reside requires three witnesses to a will. However, the state where you executed your will only requires two witnesses. When you die, the state of your last residence will admit the will to probate even though you did not have three witnesses, since the will was properly witnessed in the state where you originally signed it.

IF I AM TERMINALLY ILL OR IN A VEGETATIVE STATE, I DO NOT WANT TO BE KEPT ALIVE BY ARTIFICIAL MEANS. HOW CAN I MAKE MY FEELINGS KNOWN BEFORE SUCH A TRAGEDY OCCURS?

You can execute a "living will." The Supreme Court of the United States has ruled that all competent adults have the right to refuse medical care if they so choose, and if there is "clear and convincing" evidence that someone who is unable to communicate would have wanted to refuse medical treatment, the courts must honor those wishes.

Some states have enacted legislation to provide for health care proxies or other documents that will be deemed "clear and convincing" evidence of a person's health care wishes when properly executed; others have not.

These laws, if any, will differ from state to state. In some states, you may be able to execute a health care proxy that designates your spouse or child as the person who will speak for you in the event that you are unable to communicate your health care decisions to others. If you give this person specific written instructions (witnessed by others) as to how you would want your medical care (or lack thereof) to be handled, a court should honor your wishes.

Your living will can specify that if you are in a coma and are not expected to return from a vegetative state, all medical treatment can be withdrawn, including tube feeding of food and water. You may wish to consult with both your attorney and your doctor in preparing a living will for yourself.

WHEN SHOULD I EXECUTE A "LIVING WILL"?

Any competent adult who has specific health care decisions that he or she wishes to communicate to others should execute a living will. If you have strong feelings that you would not want to be kept alive by artificial means if you're in a terminal or vegetative state, a living will may be the only way to make sure that your wishes are carried out.

You may know of someone who went into a coma as a result of an automobile accident and has been in that condition for several years without any real hope of leading a normal life again. You may want to be sure this never happens to you. You may not want to be a monetary and/or psychological burden on your family if you should end up in such a condition. By having a living will, you can be assured that your health care wishes will be carried out.

IF MY STATE HAS NO "LIVING WILL" LAW, HOW CAN I PROTECT MYSELF BY CREATING "CLEAR AND CONVINCING PROOF" OF MY HEALTH CARE DECISIONS?

There are organizations throughout the country, including the Society for the Right to Die in New York City, which can assist you and your attorney in preparing a document that will adequately communicate your health care decisions to others. Your attorney can advise you on alternatives available to you.

IF I SHOULD BECOME TERMINALLY ILL OR IN A VEGETATIVE STATE, I WANT MY SPOUSE TO HAVE THE AUTHORITY TO MANAGE MY AFFAIRS. CAN I DO ANYTHING ABOUT THIS NOW?

A power of attorney in favor of your spouse executed today, when you are physically well and mentally alert, goes into effect immediately unless you specify otherwise. You may not want your spouse to have these extensive powers now, but only if you become physically or mentally unable to do so for yourself.

Some states now provide for a "springing" power of attorney, which allows the power of attorney to go into effect only upon the happening of a specified event (for example, incapacity of mind or body). In this way you can be assured that if you're in an automobile accident and go into a coma, your spouse will be able to gain access to your bank accounts to pay your medical bills and to take care of your day-to-day affairs.

MY MOTHER, WHO DIED LAST YEAR, IS NAMED AS A BENEFICIARY IN HER SISTER'S (MY AUNT'S) WILL. MY AUNT JUST DIED. DO I NOW INHERIT MY MOTHER'S SHARE OF MY AUNT'S ESTATE?

It depends upon the language in the will and upon the laws of your state. If your aunt's will specifically states that in the event your mother predeceases her you will inherit your mother's share, you will automatically inherit your mother's portion of your aunt's estate.

If your state's laws provide that in the event of a sister's death, the sister's share automatically goes to her children, you may inherit your mother's share in your aunt's will whether or not there is a specific provision in the will to that effect.

I AM AN ADOPTED CHILD. MY ADOPTIVE MOTHER DOESN'T HAVE A WILL. IF SHE DIES WITHOUT A WILL, DO I INHERIT A PORTION OF HER ESTATE OR AM I CUT OFF BECAUSE I AM NOT A NATURAL CHILD?

Most states have updated their laws to provide that adopted children have all the rights of natural children under estate and inheritance laws. If your adoptive parents have two natural children in addition to you, all three of you would inherit as children of your mother.

If your mother did have a will and it merely stated that all of her children would inherit, you would be legally included. If you are an adopted child, you may want to ask your lawyer about your state's laws concerning your inheritance rights.

IS IT ALWAYS GOOD TO BE A BENEFICIARY UNDER A WILL?

Imagine this scenario: Out of the blue, you're notified that you are the beneficiary in your great-uncle's will, and you've inherited his big old house. You're thrilled! You imagine selling the house and making a fortune. However, what you may not know is that the house has mortgages and liens filed against it in excess of its market value. Creditors are looking to foreclose to enforce their liens.

It's possible that your great-uncle (who doesn't seem

so great to you now) made a provision in the will that all of his debts, including the mortgages and liens, were to be paid from the rest of the estate and you were to get the house free and clear. If no such provision was made and you inherit the house, you will also inherit the problems that go along with it. So there may be times when it is not beneficial for you to be a beneficiary under a will.

MY GREAT-UNCLE'S HOUSE TURNED OUT TO BE MORE TROUBLE THAN IT WAS WORTH. MUST I ACCEPT THE BEQUEST?

You don't have to accept a bequest made to you under a will, nor do you have to accept your share of an estate of a deceased who had no will. If you decide that you don't want to accept a bequest, you can renounce your portion of the estate by filing a written renunciation with the court where the estate is being administered. Upon receiving your renunciation, the court will redivide the estate according to the terms of the will or according to local law.

WHAT IS A TRUST?

A trust is a document that provides for a person's assets to be distributed to himself or herself and/or others via a fiduciary, known as a trustee.

The trustee oversees investment of the assets of the trust and distribution of the money from the trust, according to the directions in the trust. A trust can be set up to be in effect during your lifetime and/or after your death. A trust can be revocable or irrevocable. A trust can be set up for many purposes, including giving gifts to minor children, making gifts of your assets to avoid having them being included in your estate for estate tax purposes when you die, and placing assets beyond your control for a specific amount of time so that the income from that asset will be taxed as income to the beneficiaries and not to you.

Depending upon the type of trust you set up, the trust may or may not remove assets from your ownership and control, and may have different income tax and/or estate tax consequences for you.

SHOULD I HAVE A TRUST THAT IS EFFECTIVE DURING MY LIFETIME?

Depending upon your specific needs and/or your income or estate tax bracket, you may wish to set up a trust. For instance, if you want to make gifts during your lifetime to your grandchildren, you can do so by setting up a trust. It can be a simple bank account in trust, which will show you (as the owner of the bank account) "in trust for" your grandchildren, which can be revoked by you at any time by closing the bank account. Your grandchildren will automatically inherit this money when you die; however, this money will be included in your estate for estate tax purposes after you die.

You might want a custom-drafted trust, in which you appoint another person as trustee to administer assets you contribute to the trust. You thereby relinquish all ownership and control of these assets and avoid both current income taxes on the interest as it accrues during your lifetime and estate taxes upon your death.

SHOULD I SET UP A TRUST IN MY WILL?

You can also set up a trust in your will, either to supervise distribution of assets to persons who are underage or irresponsible, and/or to take advantage of tax-saving estate tax laws.

Suppose you have a twenty-two-year-old son who is a recovering drug addict and you want to supervise distribution of money to him in the event you die. You can set up a trust for him in your will so that the only way he can get money is by asking the trustee for it or by having the trustee pay it out directly to a third party (such as for rent or other necessities). In this way you can assure yourself that your hard-earned wealth will not slip through his fingers in a few short months.

Or your attorney may suggest that in order to save estate taxes, instead of leaving your entire estate to your spouse outright, you place a portion in trust for use during her lifetime but payable to your children upon her death. In that way the trust money will not be taxed in either your estate or your spouse's estate when you die. There are many options where trusts are concerned, and you should be asking for help in deciding if a trust in your will is right for you.

CAN I SET UP A TRUST IN MY WILL TO LEAVE MY ESTATE TO MY PET CAT OR DOG?

So long as you are not cutting off any relatives (such as a spouse) who may be entitled by law to claim a portion of your estate, you can leave your estate to anyone you wish, including a pet cat or dog. If you set a trust in your will for your pets, make sure you appoint a trustee who likes your animals and who is willing to carry out your wishes. The trust should also provide for what happens upon the death of the beneficiary pet—you may wish to leave the rest to your favorite charity after your pet is gone.

I AM CONFUSED ABOUT THE DIFFERENT KINDS OF LEGAL REPRESENTATIVES. WHAT ARE THE DIFFERENCES BETWEEN A

FIDUCIARY, EXECUTOR, ADMINISTRATOR, CONSERVATOR, TRUSTEE, ATTORNEY-IN-FACT, AND A GUARDIAN?

The exact names of legal representatives may vary in your state, but here are some generally used definitions:

1. Fiduciary: A fiduciary is another name for a legal representative, which includes anyone who acts on your behalf (while you're alive or after your death), to do the things you would have done if available or capable. Executors, administrators, conservators, trustees, attorneys-in-fact, and guardians are all types of fiduciaries/legal representatives.

2. Executor or administrator: The terms "executor" and "administrator" are generally used to describe fiduciaries who act on behalf of deceased persons, either appointed in a will or by court order if there is no will. In your state, the term "executor" may describe someone who has been appointed to represent a deceased person in a will and the term "administrator" may describe someone who has been appointed other than by will (such as in the case where the designated executor in a will is too sick to accept the post, or if there is no will).

3. Conservator: The term "conservator" is used in some states to describe the person appointed by the court to act as the legal representative of a person who is alive but physically or mentally incapable of managing his or her own affairs. For instance, if your mother becomes senile and cannot take care of herself or her belongings, you may be appointed as her conservator to manage her affairs for her.

4. Trustee: The term "trustee" is used to describe a person (or an entity such as a banking institution) who is appointed by a trust document to administer

money and pay it out pursuant to specific instructions in the trust document. In your will, for example, you might set up a trust for your minor children and appoint a friend as trustee to administer your money until your children reach a certain age. Depending upon the type of trust, the trustee may act during your lifetime and/or after your death.

5. Attorney-in-fact: The term "attorney-in-fact" is used to describe a person who is appointed by another to act on his or her behalf during his or her lifetime. Say you're going to work in Europe for several years and you want someone to have the power to manage your financial affairs while you are away. You can execute a power-of-attorney document and appoint an attorney-in-fact to act in your place.

6. Guardian: A guardian is a person who has been appointed to oversee the legal rights of someone who is not capable of acting on his or her own (because they are minor children, mentally incapable, physically unable, or missing) and whose legal rights may be affected by a particular court proceeding. A guardian will usually be appointed for minor children who are named as beneficiaries in the will of a deceased person.

IF I DO NOT APPOINT A GUARDIAN FOR MY CHILDREN IN MY WILL, DOES THE STATE APPOINT A GUARDIAN FOR THEM WHEN I DIE?

If you die without having appointed a guardian for your minor children (either by having no will or by having a will that fails to appoint a guardian), someone (usually a family member or a friend) may petition the court to be appointed as guardian for your children. The court will consider the relationship of the proposed guardian with you and your children and the best interest of the children.

The surviving parent of the children will normally be given first preference to be the guardian of the children. An aunt who has a close relationship with the children will be preferred to a distant cousin who has never met them. If no one comes forward voluntarily to be a guardian, then the state will usually appoint someone to do the job.

DO I HAVE TO HAVE SOMEONE'S PERMISSION TO APPOINT HIM OR HER AS EXECUTOR OF MY WILL? IF NOT, CAN HE OR SHE REFUSE THE JOB?

You don't have to have someone's permission to appoint him as executor under your will. It's a good idea to do so, however, because if he doesn't want the job, he can decline it.

You may think that your brother is the perfect person to handle your affairs after you have died. However, he may not wish to take on the responsibility due to his own family and job commitments. If you find out now that he would prefer not to act as your executor, you can appoint someone else in your will who agrees to take on the job.

WHAT HAPPENS IF MY LEGAL REPRESENTATIVE DIES?

If you designated an alternate legal representative in your will, that person would apply to the court to take over the job. If you did not name an alternate, or if the alternate is unable or unwilling to assume the responsibility, another person can apply to the court to take over. If no one wants to take the job, the court will appoint someone (usually from a list of persons who voluntarily sign up to do this). There will always be someone who can step in and finish the job, even if it is a total stranger.

WHAT EXPENSES WILL MY HEIRS HAVE TO PAY OTHERS AFTER I DIE (AND WHAT IS LEFT OVER FOR THEM)?

The nature and the amount of expenses to administer your estate will vary from state to state. Among the expenses your estate may have to pay are the following:

1. Funeral expenses;
2. Federal estate tax, if your net estate exceeds $600,000;
3. State estate or inheritance tax (will vary from state to state);
4. Miscellaneous fees, including court filing fees, property appraisal fees, costs of preserving estate assets (e.g., cost of utilities to maintain a decedent's residence until it can be sold), attorneys' fees, and fiduciaries' commissions for managing the estate.

Certain expenses such as estate taxes, fiduciaries' commissions (usually a percentage of the estate paid to the executor or administrator to manage the estate), and court filing fees may be determined by the size of your estate; the greater the value of the estate, the greater the fee that will be paid. Other expenses will be relatively fixed, such as funeral expenses (unless your heirs decide to throw a fantastic party in your memory!).

Although your attorney will not be able to give you an exact figure as to what the amount of your expenses will be, he or she should be able to give you a "ballpark figure" as to the portion of the estate that will be consumed by taxes and administrative expenses.

I HAVE HEARD THAT I CAN SET UP A LIFETIME TRUST AND AVOID ESTATE TAXES WHEN I DIE. SHOULD I DO THIS?

If you place assets into a trust that begins during your

lifetime and that meets certain legal requirements, you may be able to exclude these assets from your estate when you die. However, you must weigh the advantages of the trust (avoiding estate taxes) versus the disadvantages, including loss of control of these assets (you must appoint a third party as the trustee to manage them) and the inability to revoke the trust once you've set it up.

You must also consider the size of your estate; if it's too small, the tax benefits may be small or even zero. If you want to set up a lifetime trust, you should probably have an estate worth at least $600,000 (the minimum amount at which federal estate taxes become payable).

Once you've set up the trust, you can't change your mind later and decide that you'd rather purchase a retirement home in Florida. You and your tax advisers can decide if a lifetime trust is a good decision for you.

ONCE I MAKE AN IRREVOCABLE LIFETIME TRUST FOR THE PURPOSES OF REMOVING ASSETS FROM MY ESTATE WHEN I DIE, CAN I CHANGE MY MIND?

If you change your mind after you've signed an irrevocable trust, there will be important tax considerations you will want to discuss with your attorney. Although you may be able to have the trustee "give back" the assets to you, the trustee may have to pay a gift tax on the transfer and thereby deplete the trust assets. Also, once the assets go back to you, they are back in your estate for estate tax purposes. Even if you sign another irrevocable trust immediately, the three-year period you must wait before an asset is considered completely out of your estate for estate tax purposes will start to run again from the date the assets left your possession and control. (If you die within the three-year waiting period, any transfer made by you will revert to your estate for the purposes of computing estate tax.) You must ask questions about the impact of trying to revoke an irrevocable trust with your attorney before you sign the trust agreement.

WILL MY ESTATE BE SUBJECT TO ESTATE TAXES OR INHERITANCE TAXES WHEN I DIE?

For federal estate tax purposes, your estate will only be taxable if all of your assets, less allowable deductions, exceeds $600,000 in value (and you have not previously used gift tax credits which would reduce the estate tax credits that you are allowed).

If your estate consists of real estate worth $150,000, bank accounts worth $70,000 and life insurance in the amount of $100,000 (for a total of $320,000), your estate will not have to pay federal estate tax when you die. If your estate exceeds $600,000, you will have to pay federal estate taxes, computed on a specific schedule; your attorney should be able to give you an estimate of the amount of federal estate taxes that will be payable by your estate.

As far as state law is concerned, your estate may be fully or partially taxable, depending upon the size of your estate. For instance, if you had the $320,000 estate in the above example, but your state allowed a credit for the first $100,000 in computing state estate or inheritance taxes, your estate or your beneficiaries would effectively pay estate taxes on only $220,000. If your estate was only $90,000 and if your state had a $100,000 credit, no estate taxes would be due. Since state laws vary, you should ask how your state's laws affect you.

WHAT IS THE DIFFERENCE BETWEEN STATE ESTATE TAX AND INHERITANCE TAX?

Usually, a state will have estate taxes or inheritance taxes, but not both. Whichever one it has determines where the tax money comes from—does the state get its money from the deceased party or from the people who inherit from him? An estate tax taxes the estate itself for assets passed from a deceased person to his or her beneficiaries. An inheritance tax taxes the beneficiaries for inheritances they receive from a deceased person.

In a state with an estate tax, the estate is legally responsible for paying the estate taxes due, and the beneficiaries may not have to contribute the taxes applicable to their shares unless there is not enough money available from other sources to do so.

In a state with an inheritance tax, the beneficiaries are legally responsible for paying the taxes on the assets they receive from a deceased person.

If you know you are named as a beneficiary in a will, it would be smart to find out whether you might be responsible for taxes when you inherit the asset.

WHAT ASSETS WILL BE SUBJECT TO ESTATE TAX WHEN I DIE?

Everything you own, either alone or jointly with another, may be subject to estate tax when you die, including real estate, stocks and bonds, cash, life insurance, automobiles, household goods and personal effects, boats, annuities, retirement plans, antiques, clothing, jewelry, and other items.

WHAT PORTION OF JOINTLY HELD ASSETS WILL BE INCLUDED IN MY ESTATE WHEN I DIE?

If you have a joint bank account with your sister, for example, the balance of that bank account will be included in your estate upon your death (unless your sister can prove that she contributed to that account, and then the amount she can prove she put in will be excluded from the gross value of your estate).

Similarly, if you own a boat jointly with your brother, the entire value of that boat will be included in your gross estate, except to the extent that your brother can prove that he paid for the boat. Also, the proceeds of life insurance policies that you own will be fully included in your gross estate. Death benefits from retirement plans will be fully taxable in your estate as well. So, in conducting your estate planning, you should be aware that all assets you own may be subject to estate tax.

WHAT HAPPENS IF MY SISTER AND/OR BROTHER AND I DIE SIMULTANEOUSLY?

The legal representatives of each estate would have to figure out which portion of your joint holdings would go into each estate, depending upon local law.

IS THERE ANY WAY I CAN AVOID HAVING ASSETS THAT I HAVE ACQUIRED OVER MY LIFETIME FROM BEING INCLUDED IN MY ESTATE FOR ESTATE TAX PURPOSES?

There are a variety of estate planning techniques that, if properly executed, will exclude an asset from your estate for federal estate tax purposes.

One such technique might be to engage in a plan of periodic gift-giving to your would-be beneficiaries. The gift will not be included in your estate if it was completed at least three years before you die. (You may, however, have to pay gift taxes on these gifts.) Suppose you have six grandchildren. You and your husband may be able to give each of them $20,000 per year tax-free, so that you can divest yourself of $120,000 per year. However, when you die, all gifts made within three years of your death will be included in your federal taxable estate.

Another tax-planning technique is to set up an irrevocable lifetime trust into which you transfer assets. You must completely divest yourself of all ownership so that you no longer have any control over the assets. For instance, if you place a life insurance policy into a lifetime trust, you make the trustee of the trust the owner of the policy, so that you no longer have the right to change the beneficiary or borrow against the cash value of the policy as you would have if you still owned the policy.

Also, by proper drafting of your will, you can set up a "unified credit trust" that takes advantage of the exclusion of approximately $600,000 from your gross federal estate. For instance, if you set up a unified credit trust that directs that during your spouse's lifetime the income goes to him, but upon his death, the balance of the trust goes to your children, you have effectively prevented the balance of this trust from being included in your husband's estate when he dies, and you have avoided any federal estate tax on the sum of money placed in this trust.

The above discussion may or may not be applicable to your state estate tax or inheritance laws, so you should ask your attorney to explain your possible options to you.

I HAVE A BANK ACCOUNT THAT IS IN TRUST FOR MY NIECE. DO I HAVE TO SPECIFICALLY MENTION THIS ACCOUNT IN MY WILL, OR DOES SHE AUTOMATICALLY GET THIS MONEY?

A bank account in trust for your niece will go directly

to her upon your death, whether you mention it in your will or not.

Any assets that are owned by you "in trust for" another person (bank accounts, life insurance, pension plans, etc.), payable upon death, will bypass the will and go directly instead to the designated person without having to wait for the will to be probated in court.

Assets that are owned solely by you with no directly designated beneficiary or co-owner (such as bank accounts in your name only, solely owned real estate, and any items of value you wish to pass on), will be distributed according to your will.

MY SISTER JUST DIED UNEXPECTEDLY. MY MOTHER, WHO IS STILL ALIVE, HAD JOINT BANK ACCOUNTS WITH HER SO SHE COULD HELP MY MOTHER MANAGE HER AFFAIRS. THESE BANK ACCOUNTS CONTAINED MY MOTHER'S MONEY ONLY. THE ESTATE TAX PEOPLE NOW WANT TO INCLUDE THE FULL VALUE OF THE JOINTLY HELD ASSETS IN THE ESTATE OF MY SISTER, EVEN THOUGH THE MONEY WAS ALL EARNED AND OWNED BY MY MOTHER. CAN THEY DO THIS?

Unless you can prove otherwise, estate tax authorities generally presume that a jointly held account was owned in full by the first person to die, because the law allows them to do so. You would have to prove that the money all belonged to your mother (perhaps by showing that the funds originated in a bank account solely owned by your mother) in order to exclude the jointly held assets from your sister's estate.

You should gather all of your mother's records together, locate the source of each jointly held asset with your sister (was your mother's house sold and the proceeds deposited into the joint account?), and submit the proof together with your sister's estate tax return.

HOW LONG SHOULD I HOLD ON TO RECORDS (AND WHAT RECORDS SHOULD I KEEP) PROVING I CONTRIBUTED TO A JOINTLY HELD ACCOUNT SO IF MY CO-OWNER DIES FIRST, THE WHOLE VALUE WON'T BE TAXED IN HIS ESTATE?

Keep deposit slips, copies of checks, income tax records, and other documents that prove the amount you contributed to the joint account. Keep these records as soon as you open the account and continue to keep these records until either you or your co-owner dies. There is no magic time period after which you no longer have to keep records in this case.

MY GRANDFATHER LEFT $1 MILLION IN TRUST FOR ME UNDER HIS WILL. THE MONEY WAS MISMANAGED BY THE TRUSTEE, WHICH WAS A BANK. THE FUNDS WERE REDUCED TO ALMOST NOTHING. DO I AS A BENEFICIARY HAVE ANY RECOURSE AGAINST THE BANK TRUSTEE?

You have the right to demand an accounting of what happened to all the money in your trust. An accounting will tell you what the original balance of the money was, what happened in the meantime (were there payouts made or interest earned, or were there investments sold and new investments purchased?) and what is left.

If after you receive the accounting you believe the bank did not act as a "reasonable person" in managing your trust funds, you have the right to sue the bank to be reimbursed for money that was not properly managed by the bank. The "reasonable person" rule requires that trustees manage funds in the same manner as a prudent person of ordinary intelligence might with his or her funds. So, if the bank invested all of the trust funds in high-risk stocks and the stocks became worthless, you would be able to make a claim against the bank, since the bank, as a prudent investor, should have invested the trust funds in a combination of low-risk, medium-risk, and high-risk invest-ments. However, if the bank placed your assets in proper investments and then the stock market crashed, the bank cannot be held responsible for the losses.

IS THERE ANY WAY I CAN ASSURE PROPER MANAGEMENT OF MY MONEY AFTER I DIE?

Choose a person you trust and who has good business judgment to handle your money. You may love your sister, but when it comes to money, she may be totally irresponsi-ble and be unable to manage your financial affairs compe-tently. If she is your only relative, you may consider asking a trusted adviser, such as your accountant, to handle your affairs after you die. You can also put provisions in your will that prohibit your fiduciary from investing in high-risk investments. Some states' laws automatically prohibit your fiduciary from choosing to place your money in high-risk situations, unless you specifically allow it under your will.

MY MOTHER HAS BECOME MENTALLY (OR PHYSICALLY) INCAPABLE OF MANAGING HER OWN AFFAIRS. HOW CAN I BE APPOINTED AS HER REPRESENTATIVE TO MANAGE HER AFFAIRS?

If your mother executed a power of attorney while she was competent, which specifically stated that if she became incompetent, the power of attorney would still be effective, and which appointed you as her representa-tive, you'll be able to handle her affairs in the same man-ner as if your mother were doing it herself.

However, if your mother did not execute such a power of attorney, you can petition the court to be appointed as a conservator of your mother's person and property. As conservator, you'll be able to legally manage all her affairs, including withdrawing money from her bank account to pay bills, buying or selling real estate or other assets, and handling business dealings with others.

If your mother became physically unable to live at home and had to be put in a nursing home, and you were appointed as her conservator, you could sell her house as her representative and open a bank account to put the money in. You could then use the money from her bank account to pay the nursing-home bills, medical bills, and other obligations. If your mother owned a valuable antique car that she had contracted to sell to a collector, you would be able to sign over the title to the car to the collector and complete the sale. These and many other day-to-day situations could be managed by you on behalf of your mother if you are appointed as her conservator.

MY FATHER IS NINETY-TWO YEARS OLD AND HEALTHY. IF HE LATER BECOMES ILL AND HAS TO GO INTO A NURSING HOME, HOW CAN WE PREVENT ALL OF HIS ASSETS FROM BEING DEPLETED IN PAYING FOR THE NURSING-HOME COSTS?

If your father has little or no income and few assets, he may be eligible for Medicare when he goes into a nursing home. However, if he has substantial assets and a good income from the assets at the time he goes into the nursing home, he won't be able to receive Medicare benefits. What most families elect to do is to transfer assets from the elderly person's name into another's name, such as a younger family member.

Medicare does require that a certain minimum amount of time must elapse between the time of the transfer of the asset and the application for Medicare coverage, currently thirty months. So it pays to plan ahead, with your attorney and tax adviser, if you have an elderly relative whom you expect may need institutional care in the near future.

WE WERE INFORMED BY THE NURSING HOME WHERE WE WANT TO PLACE OUR FATHER THAT THEY WOULD NOT ACCEPT HIM UNLESS HIS CHILDREN WOULD GUARANTEE PAYMENT OF HIS BILLS. ARE WE LEGALLY OBLIGATED TO DO SO?

Although parents have a legal obligation to support their minor-age children, generally children do not have a reciprocal obligation to support their parents in their old age.

If your parent is poverty-stricken and must apply for public assistance, the laws of your state may burden you with the obligation of support if you have the ability to pay. Otherwise, unless you agree in writing to guarantee payment of your father's nursing home bills, you cannot be held legally responsible for this debt, either before or after he dies. The nursing-home operators are trying to get you to guarantee payment of the debt so that if the assets of your father's estate are insufficient, they will have someone to fall back on to pay the difference between the value of the assets and the actual amount of the unpaid bills. If you have no other choice (for instance, no other nursing home will accept your father except on similar conditions), you may have to guarantee the debt (or find someone who will) if you want a place for your father to live.

MY MOTHER HAD A LARGE BALANCE ON HER CREDIT CARDS WHEN SHE RECENTLY DIED. WHO IS RESPONSIBLE FOR PAYING OFF THESE DEBTS?

Your mother's estate is legally responsible for paying off debts she accrued during her lifetime. In the case of credit cards or installment loans, you should check with the credit card companies or the lender to see whether your mother purchased credit life insurance as part of her monthly payments, which would automatically pay off the balance, if any, on the credit card debt or the loan when she died.

The credit card companies, as creditors of the estate, can file a claim against the estate for any balance due. If the assets in your mother's estate are enough to pay off her debts, her assets will be sold and these debts will be paid off as a part of administering the estate. If there are insufficient assets to pay off these balances, the credit card company can look to a cosigner on the credit card, if any, to pay the balance. If there are not enough assets to pay the balances and no cosigner, the credit card company is out of luck, since you, as her next of kin, cannot be held responsible for your mother's debts unless you agreed to do so in writing.

MY MOTHER JUST TURNED SIXTY-FIVE AND STILL EARNS AN INCOME. HOW MUCH MONEY CAN SHE LEGALLY EARN WITHOUT JEOPARDIZING HER SOCIAL SECURITY PAYMENTS?

The Social Security Administration has a maximum income a person may earn before social security payments are reduced. You may earn up to that figure without any reduction of your social security payments. The maximum changes from time to time. Also, there is a certain age beyond which you may earn unlimited income and still receive full social security benefits.

It makes sense to consult your attorney or your local social security office to determine what your options may be at your particular age. If your mother wants to work beyond age sixty-five and is earning more than the maximum, she may choose to continue to work and not to apply for social security payments until she is older. Then, if she decides to retire at a later date, she will be entitled to higher social security payments per month

than if she had retired at age sixty-five (because she
started drawing money out at a later age). Or, if she
reaches the age at which she may earn unlimited income
without penalty, she can both earn income and collect
social security benefits.

HOW DO I KNOW IF MY ELDERLY PARENT QUALIFIES FOR MEDICARE?

You can contact your local Medicare office or your
attorney to get Medicare's current eligibility requirements. Your elderly parent may be able to receive a small
income and also hold some assets and still be eligible to
receive Medicare payments. Your elderly parent may also
be able to place assets in trust for family members' benefit and still be eligible to receive payments. Different
states have different eligibility requirements, so it may
pay to have your elderly parent establish a residence in
another state in anticipation of a better level of payments.

SECTION 11

THE LAW ON YOUR SIDE: SMART QUESTIONS TO ASK ABOUT ATTORNEYS' ETHICS AND BEHAVIOR

If a lawyer behaves in a manner that seems wrong or unethical, it's your right to confront her about it.

Ask her why she took such an action—or refused to take an action you think appropriate. If her answer does not satisfy you, you may want to check with another attorney to see if he agrees with you or with your attorney.

The law is complicated, and is constantly changing. It's difficult for lawyers to keep up, and it's even more difficult for us to know all about the law. You may think that your lawyer is doing something wrong when really he's acting according to a new, or rewritten, law. You'll never know if you don't ask questions. If your lawyer won't answer your questions, you may want to get another lawyer.

There is no reason for an attorney to keep secrets from you. You have the right to know exactly what is being done about your legal problems. You have a right to see correspondence, you have the right to know what strategies your lawyer is planning, and you have the right to a strict accounting of how and for what you are being billed. And you have the right to question anything your lawyer does.

IF I TELL SOMETHING TO MY ATTORNEY, MUST HE KEEP IT CONFIDENTIAL?

Under most circumstances, an attorney is bound by the law and ethical codes to keep information disclosed to him confidential and not disclose it to anyone else without your consent.

However, there are some exceptions to that rule. If you tell your attorney you intend to commit a crime, your attorney has a duty to inform the authorities and to give them any information that might assist in the prevention of that crime. So, if you consult with your attorney and inform him of your intent to commit tax fraud, he'll have a duty to inform the applicable tax authorities. He'll have to disclose any information to them that could prevent the crime from being committed.

Another exception is when a court order is issued directing your attorney to disclose otherwise confidential matters. Suppose you tell your attorney you're taking an extended "vacation" in Mexico—when in reality you've embezzled $1 million from your employer and are going south to avoid prosecution. If a court order is later issued, your attorney will be compelled to disclose your whereabouts to the authorities.

IF MY ATTORNEY'S SECRETARY OVERHEARS A CONVERSATION WHEN I AM DIVULGING CONFIDENTIAL INFORMATION, IS THE SECRETARY ALSO BOUND TO KEEP MY CONFIDENCES SECRET?

It's part of a lawyer's duty to exercise reasonable care that her employees and associates do not divulge any confidential information overheard by them or known to them in the performance of their duties. Normally, when an employee is hired, an attorney will make it clear to the employee that a condition of holding the job is that all client information must remain a secret, and if this confidence is broken, it will be grounds for dismissal.

WILL THE ATTORNEY OF MY CHOICE ALWAYS BE ABLE TO REPRESENT ME?

Not if there are ethical considerations that prevent the attorney from accepting you as a client. There can be any number of reasons for the lawyer to decline to represent you, including:

- Your attorney's business, financial, or personal interests conflict with your interests. If your attorney is also a real-estate broker, for example, he may have to refuse to represent you in the sale of your house. There could be a possible conflict between his interest as real-estate broker (entitled to a broker's commission only if the deal closes) and his role as attorney (which may require him to refuse to close the deal if the circumstances are detrimental to you).
- Your interests conflict with those of an existing client. For instance, if your attorney regularly represents a client whom you intend to sue for breach of contract, she cannot represent you in that lawsuit because of her ongoing business relationship with your intended adversary.
- The attorney you wish to retain will probably be

called as a material witness in your case. Suppose you and your attorney are lunching together in a quiet little café in town. While the two of you are dining, someone who looks a lot like you robs a local bank; later on, you're picked up and charged with the robbery. Since your attorney's testimony that you were having lunch together at the time would have substantial impact on the case, he would be obligated to refuse to act as counsel for you in this criminal matter.

IF MY ATTORNEY CAN'T REPRESENT ME ON A PARTICULAR MATTER BECAUSE OF ETHICAL CONSIDERATIONS, CAN I HAVE A MEMBER OF HIS LAW FIRM REPRESENT ME?

If your attorney can't represent you because of ethical prohibitions, it's possible that no member or associate of his firm can do so, either.

What if your attorney refuses to represent you because he has confidential information (from a former job) about your prospective adversary? No member of his law firm can undertake to represent you unless he, as the disqualified lawyer, effectively screens himself from any participation in, or sharing of, the fees in that particular case. In some states, even these precautions may not be enough to allow the firm to represent you.

If your lawyer is in a large firm where it would be easy to screen himself, there should be no ethical prohibition against someone else in the firm representing you. However, if your attorney is practicing in a small office with only one other attorney and a shared secretary, he may feel that effective screening from your case is not possible and decline to accept your case.

ONE OF MY FRIENDS TOLD ME THAT HER LAWYER HAD ADMITTED TO HER THAT HE WAS NOT QUALIFIED TO PRACTICE LAW IN MY STATE SINCE HE HAD NEVER PASSED THE BAR EXAM. I TOLD THIS TO MY LAWYER. MY LAWYER TOLD ME SHE HAD A DUTY TO "TURN IN" THIS UNQUALIFIED ATTORNEY TO THE AUTHORITIES IF IT WAS TRUE. DOES AN ATTORNEY HAVE A DUTY TO "RAT" ON HIS OR HER FELLOW ATTORNEYS?

Just as certain institutions, such as military academies, have codes of conduct that require a member to inform the authorities if another member has broken a rule, your attorney may have a duty to report a breach or a possible breach of an attorney's code of ethics. This is part of a process of self-policing through which the bar organizations will censure or disbar members who commit breaches of ethics rules or state laws regulating the practice of attorneys.

If the other lawyer was in fact unqualified to practice law in your state, your lawyer would have a duty to report him to the applicable authority, whether it be the local bar association or a court disciplinary committee. If your lawyer did not report such a breach, she could be subject to disciplinary proceedings.

WHEN I WAS AT A COCKTAIL PARTY, I WAS DISCUSSING A PROBLEM I WAS HAVING WITH ONE OF MY UNION EMPLOYEES. AN ATTORNEY, WHO OVERHEARD THE CONVERSATION, CHIMED IN AND SUGGESTED THAT I RETAIN LEGAL COUNSEL. HOWEVER, WHEN I ASKED FOR HER BUSINESS CARD SO THAT I COULD RETAIN HER AS COUNSEL, SHE SAID SHE COULD NOT ETHICALLY DO SO. WHY IS THAT?

Under most circumstances, a lawyer who offers you unsolicited legal advice is prohibited from accepting employment resulting from that unsolicited advice. There are exceptions:

1. The attorney is a relative or friend of yours. If the attorney was your aunt Bertha or your close friend Myrtle, she could properly give you unsolicited advice and then accept the employment stemming from that advice without violation of any ethical rule.
2. You are an existing client of the attorney (even on an unrelated matter). Then the attorney would be able to accept the assignment from you.

I ATTENDED A SEMINAR GIVEN BY AN ATTORNEY ON ESTATE PLANNING AND WILLS. AT THE END OF THE SEMINAR, I ASKED HIM WHETHER HE WOULD PREPARE AN ESTATE PLAN FOR ME AND DRAFT MY WILL. HE AGREED TO DO SO. IS THIS ETHICAL?

In most states an attorney may accept employment gained as a result of his participation in a program to educate the public as to their rights, how to properly select an attorney, or how to find and use legal services.

Similarly, the lawyer may be able to accept employment resulting from speeches or writing, so long as the speeches or writing don't offer individual advice. So, if after that attorney's generalized seminar you became interested in retaining that attorney, he would be able to accept your case without breaking any ethical rules.

MY ATTORNEY AND I WANT TO START UP A PUBLISHING BUSINESS TOGETHER. CAN WE ETHICALLY DO SO?

As long as your business does not consist of the practice of law, you'll be able to start a business together. First, however, your attorney will have to present a full disclosure of all possible adverse interests that might compromise his professional judgment as your counsel.

Suppose your attorney is drafting up an agreement between himself and you. Acting as your attorney, he should officially advise you that you and he may have conflicting interests and that you may wish to retain another attorney to represent you. If you decide that you still want him to represent you, after full disclosure, he can still act as your attorney without any ethical problem.

I AM BUYING MY MOTHER'S HOUSE FROM HER. CAN MY ATTORNEY REPRESENT BOTH ME AND MY MOTHER (SINCE WE ALL AGREE ON ALL THE TERMS OF THE CONTRACT)?

Although it's generally preferable to have an independent attorney represent each side of a potentially adversarial situation, it may be permissible and appropriate in some circumstances to have one attorney represent both sides in a matter.

If you and your mother genuinely see eye to eye on all terms of the sale of the house, and both you and your mother sign letters agreeing that the attorney will represent both sides, the attorney may be permitted to represent both sides in this transaction. Before agreeing to represent both sides of any matter, your attorney must disclose to you that you have the right to seek independent counsel and that he can only continue to represent both of you so long as no conflicts of interest arise.

I FOUND OUT THAT THE LAWYER I HIRED TO REPRESENT ME IN MY DIVORCE ACTION IS THE BROTHER OF MY WIFE'S ATTORNEY. THE ATTORNEYS ARE FROM DIFFERENT LAW FIRMS. CAN WE BOTH KEEP OUR ATTORNEYS?

If the attorneys are both of the opinion that the proper representation of their respective clients will not be compromised by the fact that they are also brothers, and each of the clients consents to the representation after full disclosure, there should be no ethical problem. It's possible, however, that your attorney prefers not to take a case where his brother is opposing counsel. If so, he may recommend you find someone else to represent you.

I'M HAVING A DISPUTE WITH THE INTERNAL REVENUE SERVICE. I WENT TO SEE AN ATTORNEY WHO USED TO WORK FOR THE IRS, BECAUSE I THOUGHT SHE WOULD BE THE BEST PERSON TO REPRESENT ME. AFTER I EXPLAINED MY PROBLEM TO HER, SHE SAID SHE HAD TO DECLINE MY CASE BECAUSE SHE HAD WORKED ON MY MATTER WHILE SHE WAS EMPLOYED BY THE IRS. WHY IS THIS SO?

Attorneys have an obligation to avoid impropriety, or even the possible appearance of impropriety. The ethical guidelines of her state may prohibit her from working on any matter in her private law practice that she worked on while she was a government employee. She might have had access to confidential government records while working on your matter that would conflict with her prospective obligation to you if she took you on as a client.

As an example: While working for the IRS, this attorney had access to several of your past years' income tax returns. There were some slight irregularities that the IRS chose to overlook in favor of pursuing you for one particular year on a large item they wished to disallow. The attorney may know that if you obtain a ruling in your favor in tax court on this item, the IRS intends to pursue the previously overlooked items, and this might color her judgment if she undertook to represent you. If this were the case, she could not divulge this confidential information to you; she could only say that she won't take you as a client because she worked on your case while an IRS employee.

I AM PURCHASING AN OUT-OF-STATE VACATION HOME. CAN MY IN-STATE ATTORNEY REPRESENT ME OR DO I HAVE TO RETAIN OUT-OF-STATE COUNSEL?

Legally, attorneys are qualified to practice law only in the states in which they've been admitted to the bar. If an attorney wants to practice law in another state, he or she must study the law of that state and meet the admission requirements. This usually means successfully passing the bar exam of that particular state and complying with practical experience qualifications, if any. There is no country-wide registration system by which attorneys can become qualified to practice law in another state.

If you want your in-state attorney to represent you in an out-of-state matter, however, he may be able to do so, provided he takes certain action. For instance, he can retain out-of-state counsel to officially represent you in the out-of-state transaction, and he can act as an intermediary between you and the out-of-state counsel. This may be accomplished with a series of long-distance telephone calls between your in-state and out-of-state attorneys. Or, in special circumstances, your attorney may be able to be admitted to the bar of the other state for the purposes of that case only, if the court permits.

I'M INVOLVED IN A DISPUTE WITH THE CONTRACTOR WHO PUT AN ADDITION ON MY HOUSE. THE CONTRACTOR IS REPRESENTED BY AN ATTORNEY, BUT HIS ATTORNEY IS OUT OF TOWN AND CAN'T BE REACHED. WHY DID MY ATTORNEY REFUSE TO SPEAK WITH THE CONTRACTOR DIRECTLY?

Attorneys have ethical obligations when communicating with your adversaries. Your state may specifically prohibit communication with the contractor unless the contractor's attorney consents in advance. If no such permission is given and your attorney goes ahead and calls the contractor, the contractor or his attorney can file a formal complaint with the local bar association.

MY NEIGHBOR'S DOG KEEPS DIGGING UP MY FLOWER BED. I WANT TO BRING A LAWSUIT AGAINST THE NEIGHBOR. MY ATTORNEY REFUSES TO START THE LAWSUIT FOR ME. AS LONG AS I'M WILLING TO PAY HIM, WHAT'S THE DIFFERENCE WHY I WANT TO SUE?

Your attorney has an ethical obligation to refuse to start or continue to participate in lawsuits that are brought merely to harass or maliciously injure another person. Digging up your flower bed is not all that serious. It would be unethical for your attorney to start a lawsuit on your behalf for punitive (punishment) damages asking $50,000 for your alleged psychic injury. If you want to bring a small claims suit against your neighbor for the cost of the flowers you had to replace, that would be fine; however, if you want your attorney to start a lawsuit, you'd better be able to show a good reason for going ahead.

Otherwise, if the lawsuit is started and it turns out to be malicious or frivolous, the laws of your state may provide for fines and penalties to be assessed against you by the court.

I SAW AN ADVERTISEMENT IN THE YELLOW PAGES OF MY TELEPHONE BOOK STATING THAT A LOCAL ATTORNEY HANDLED DIVORCES. DOES THAT MEAN SHE IS A SPECIALIST IN THAT AREA?

Just because someone advertises that she handles divorce cases doesn't mean that she's a specialist in that area. Generally, attorneys are permitted to advertise that they practice a certain type of law or that they limit their practices to certain areas of the law. However, this does not guarantee that they are well experienced in that area. You as a prospective client should do your own investigation (by interviewing the attorney and/or asking friends or relatives) to ascertain the experience level of a particular attorney. In some states attorneys can be certified as specialists and are allowed to advertise as such if they meet the qualifications and pass the necessary tests. However, not every state has a such a certification process, and advertising in those states as a specialist is unethical or illegal.

IN MY LOCAL NEWSPAPER I SAW AN ADVERTISEMENT BY AN ATTORNEY WHO ADVERTISED WILLS FOR FIFTY DOLLARS. HOWEVER, AFTER I MADE THE APPOINTMENT WITH THE ATTORNEY TO DRAFT MY WILL, HE TOLD ME THAT THE PRICE WOULD BE A HUNDRED DOLLARS. CAN I FORCE HIM TO HOLD TO THE CHEAPER PRICE?

That depends. Exactly what did the ad say? The ad might have said "Simple Wills: $50." If, after meeting with you, the attorney concludes that because of your $6 million estate you should have a will including sophisticated tax planning clauses, he can properly propose a higher fee for additional legal work not included in the price for a "simple" will.

Was there an expiration date in the ad? If it stated that the price was good for thirty days from the date of the advertisement, you're out of luck if you wait more than thirty days. If there was no expiration date published, the rules of your state may specify that the lawyer must hold this price for a "reasonable amount of time" after the publication, but no less than ninety days. So, if the ad states that the price for a "simple" will is fifty dollars, and yours is a "simple" will, and you visit the attorney's office within ninety days, you can insist upon the fifty-dollar price as advertised.

I THINK MY ATTORNEY CHARGED ME AN EXCESSIVE FEE FOR THE SERVICES PERFORMED. IS THERE ANYTHING I CAN DO ABOUT IT?

Before you begin to work with any attorney, you should ask how fees are computed, and what's included in the services provided. If you think you've been charged an excessive fee, ask him to explain these issues again to make sure you're both interpreting fees in the same way. Make sure you get an itemized bill to prevent any further misunderstandings.

If you're still convinced the fees were excessive, you may have the right to file a formal complaint with the local bar association or with the local government agency that regulates the behavior of attorneys. An investigation will be held. If the attorney is found to have, in fact, charged an excessive fee, he may be formally censured or, if this is a repeated offense, possibly disbarred. You may also be able to start a lawsuit against the attorney to recover any excessive portion of the fee you may have already paid.

I OWE MY ATTORNEY A LEGAL FEE AND HE'S STARTED A LAWSUIT AGAINST ME TO COLLECT THE AMOUNT DUE. WON'T HE BE PROHIBITED FROM TESTIFYING AGAINST ME, SINCE EVERYTHING I TOLD HIM IS PROTECTED UNDER THE ATTORNEY-CLIENT PRIVILEGE?

You can't completely hide behind the attorney-client privilege if you have failed to pay your legal fees. Your attorney is permitted to divulge the nature and content of confidential communications and secrets to the extent necessary to support a claim for collection of an unpaid fee. So if your attorney represented you on a matrimonial matter, he can testify that you retained him to start a divorce action for you, explain what legal services he performed, and the amount of the fee agreed upon and earned. However, he would not be permitted to divulge the details of the extramarital affairs you disclosed to him while he was representing you, since these details would not be necessary for him to document his claim for unpaid legal fees.

I FIRED MY ATTORNEY, BUT SHE TOLD ME SHE WOULD TURN OVER MY FILES TO MY NEW ATTORNEY ONLY AFTER I HAD PAID HER LEGAL BILL IN FULL. IS THIS UNETHICAL?

Your attorney may be entitled by law to retain an "attorney's lien" on your case records and legally refuse to turn them over to you or your new attorney until you have paid her in full. If you decide in the middle of a case that you want to switch to another lawyer, you're obliged to pay the first attorney's fee in full before you'll be allowed to transfer your records to your second attorney.

Similarly, if you're in the middle of a case and you have not yet paid your attorney, despite his repeated requests, he will probably be able to apply to the court to be removed as your attorney on the grounds of nonpayment. If you pay your attorney a retainer with a $500 check that bounces twice, and you refuse to return his telephone calls about this money, he can apply to the court to withdraw from the case on the grounds that you failed to live up to a legal fee obligation.

You can always get another attorney; however, your former attorney will not release your files unless his fee is paid. If you don't need your files, you can avoid paying the fee until the first lawyer sues you for it.

I GAVE MY ATTORNEY FUNDS THAT BELONG TO ME FOR SAFEKEEPING. DO THEY HAVE TO BE KEPT IN A SPECIAL BANK ACCOUNT?

All funds that do not belong to an attorney must be placed in an "escrow" or "trust" bank account (meaning that the money does not belong to the attorney) which is separate from the attorney's other bank accounts.

If you are the purchaser in a real-estate transaction, for example, and you give the seller's attorney your $20,000 down payment to hold for safekeeping, the attorney must place this money in her escrow or trust bank account. She is forbidden to deposit this into any other bank account where the funds would become commingled with other funds (such as her business operating account).

DO MY FUNDS HAVE TO BE KEPT IN A SEPARATE ACCOUNT FROM ALL OTHER CLIENTS' FUNDS?

At any one time your attorney's trust account may hold funds from several different clients. However, she must keep careful records as to what money belongs to which client on which legal matter. For instance, if you had given your attorney $1,000 to hold as security for performance of a contract you had made, and $4,000 to pay for your wife's legal fees in a divorce action you're involved in, the attorney's records must specify which money is applicable to which matter, and for which client.

The money in your attorney's trust account is only as safe as the integrity of the attorney who is managing it. Make sure you leave your money in the hands of the right person by asking smart questions when choosing an attorney.

WILL THE MONEY I PLACE IN MY ATTORNEY'S ESCROW ACCOUNT BE EARNING INTEREST WHILE IT IS THERE?

The laws of each state differ as to whether or not you're entitled to earn interest on funds held in your attorney's escrow account. Your state may mandate that all attorney's escrow accounts bear interest—but that all of the interest in this account is to be turned over each month to the state, which will use the money to fund legal services for the poor.

The laws of your state may give an attorney the option, however, to place your trust funds in a separate interest-bearing account, with all of the interest eventually going to you. If you're giving an attorney money to be placed in trust for a long period of time, ask the attorney whether he will open a separate interest-bearing bank account in trust for you, from which you will earn the interest. This may not be worthwhile if your attorney is to hold the money for only a short period of time (unless there is a great deal of money involved). However, if even a small sum of money is to be held for an extended period of time (for instance, over a year), it could be beneficial to you to ask to have the money placed in a separate interest-bearing trust account.

THE LAW FIRM IN WHICH MY ATTORNEY WAS PRACTICING BROKE UP AND MY ATTORNEY RETIRED WHILE STILL HOLDING MY ESCROW FUNDS IN THE FIRM'S ESCROW ACCOUNT. WHAT HAPPENS TO MY MONEY?

Upon the dissolution of a law firm, at least one attorney must maintain the escrow or trust account formerly kept by the firm so that all clients' money in the account will be protected. If all of the attorneys in the dissolved firm intend to retire, a successor attorney or law firm must be found to maintain the escrow account. All clients who have money in the account should be notified in writing where the money will be deposited when the former law firm's trust account is closed and the money moved to another trust account. (The money is not returned to you because it is in escrow.) If you hire another attorney, she can arrange for your trust funds to be transferred to her trust account.

WHAT HAPPENS IF A CLIENT FOR WHOM AN ATTORNEY IS HOLDING FUNDS IN ESCROW DISAPPEARS?

If an attorney who is holding trust funds for a client cannot locate that client, she must apply for a court order directing payment of her fees and disbursements to her, and the balance to the clerk of the court to hold on behalf of the client. So, if a client disappears leaving $5,000 in escrow in an attorney's account, and the attorney is owed $1,000 in legal fees, the attorney will apply for a court order authorizing payment to herself of her $1,000 legal fee and directing the payment of the $4,000 balance to the clerk of the court to hold for the client in case he or she eventually shows up. Local law will determine how long this money must be held and what happens to it if the client never shows up.

WHAT BOOKKEEPING RECORDS IS MY ATTORNEY REQUIRED TO KEEP AND FOR HOW LONG?

Attorneys are required to maintain complete records of their transactions with clients, including records of all deposits and withdrawals for all bank accounts (including the escrow account), copies of retainer agreements, copies of bills and statements to clients, copies of records showing payments to others not in the regular employ of the attorney for services rendered by them, and checkbooks, bank statements, canceled checks, and deposit slips. Attorneys may be required to keep these records on file for a number of years, depending upon the rules of your state.

MY ATTORNEY DOESN'T HANDLE DIVORCE CASES, SO I ASKED HIM TO RECOMMEND ANOTHER ATTORNEY WHO COULD HANDLE MY DIVORCE FOR ME. I LATER FOUND OUT THAT THE MATRIMONIAL ATTORNEY HAD PAID A PORTION OF MY FEE TO MY REGULAR ATTORNEY. IS THIS ETHICAL?

Each jurisdiction has its own rules about fee-splitting arrangements between attorneys. Your state's rules may prohibit fee splitting by attorneys unless:
1. The attorneys are associates or partners; or
2. All three of the following conditions are met:

- Full disclosure has been made to the client that the legal fee will be split and the client agrees to the arrangement.
- The proportions of the fee paid to each lawyer represents the proportions of work done by each on that matter (or the lawyers may agree in writing to be jointly responsible for the case).
- The total fee is not excessive for the services provided.

In the above example, it is possible that your attorney assisted the other attorney in working on your case, such as by preparing an accounting of your assets and liabilities or by performing other services (such as legal research). However, if your state followed the above rules, you should have been notified of this arrangement and agreed to it in advance.

I REFERRED ONE OF MY FRIENDS TO MY ATTORNEY ON A LEGAL MATTER. IN MY BUSINESS, IT'S CUSTOMARY TO ASK FOR A REFERRAL FEE. WHY DID MY ATTORNEY SAY IT WAS UNETHICAL FOR HER TO GIVE ME A REFERRAL FEE?

Lawyers are prohibited from splitting legal fees with nonlawyers, so a lawyer would not ethically be able to give you a fee for referring new business to her. There are usually only narrow exceptions to the rule, such as payments by a lawyer to the estate of his deceased partner pursuant to a buyout agreement, payments to a deceased lawyer's estate by a lawyer who finished a legal matter started by another lawyer (to the extent the deceased lawyer provided services prior to his death), or payments to nonlawyer employees of a law firm under a retirement plan. Lawyers may also be prohibited from giving referral fees to each other, except to the extent the referring attorney actually worked on the case or agreed to be jointly responsible for its outcome.

MY ATTORNEY PREPARED A LEGAL BRIEF TO BE SUBMITTED TO THE COURT ON MY BEHALF. I WAS DISTURBED TO SEE THAT HE INCLUDED LAW CASES THAT OPPOSE MY POSITION. WHY DID HE INCLUDE THESE OPPOSING CASES?

The laws and ethical code of your state may require that your attorney disclose opposing law to the judge who will be ruling on your matter. For instance, if you are suing for breach of contract and there is a case having a similar set of facts to yours that rules against you, your attorney may have a duty to disclose the existence of this case to the judge.

However, after disclosing this adverse case, your attorney will try to argue either: (a) that the facts of the other case are different enough so the outcome should be different for you; or (b) the law set up by this adverse case should not be followed (for a good reason).

IF I AM ACCUSED OF A CRIME, DOES THE PROSECUTING ATTORNEY HAVE A DUTY TO DISCLOSE EVIDENCE THAT WILL BE IN MY FAVOR?

The prosecuting attorney in your criminal matter may have the obligation to make a timely disclosure to you or your attorney of all evidence that may tend to reduce the charges against you or suggest that you are not guilty.

Suppose you are accused of raping a young girl, and a DNA analysis of your semen does not match the semen obtained as evidence from the girl. Even if there is other overwhelming evidence that you were the perpetrator, this information must be disclosed to you so you can use it in your defense.

If it is not disclosed to you, you can request a retrial of your case.

I AM INVOLVED IN A BIG TRIAL AND I WANT TO GET AS MUCH PUBLICITY OUT OF IT AS POSSIBLE TO PROMOTE MY BUSINESS INTERESTS. HOWEVER, WHENEVER THE PRESS ARRIVES, MY ATTORNEY CLAMS UP AND ONLY GIVES THE BARE MINIMUM ANSWERS TO THE REPORTERS' QUESTIONS. WHY IS THIS?

Your attorney may be following the ethical rules of your state. She may be barred from disclosing any information that may be considered prejudicial to the proceeding, such as the names of witnesses, comments on the character of your adversary, your adversary's prior criminal record, the refusal or failure of your adversary to submit to a test, the results of any such test, or any opinion as to the merits of the case.

Similarly, your attorney can't disclose any information that won't be admissible at trial and that would be prejudicial to your opponent. So your attorney could not relate a story told by one of your witnesses if the story would prejudice your opponent's case.

I JUST HIRED AN ATTORNEY TO DEFEND ME IN A CRIMINAL CASE IN WHICH I AM ACCUSED OF ATTEMPTED MURDER OF TWO YOUTHS WHO ATTACKED ME IN THE SUBWAY. I HAVE NO MONEY TO PAY AN ATTORNEY UP FRONT TO HANDLE MY CRIMINAL CASE, SO I OFFERED MY ATTORNEY A HALF INTEREST IN THE LITERARY OR MEDIA RIGHTS TO MY STORY IN EXCHANGE FOR LEGAL SERVICES. SHE TOLD ME SHE COULDN'T ACCEPT PAYMENT IN THAT MANNER. WHY NOT?

Although attorneys may have certain business relationships with their clients, other business relationships are prohibited by law or ethical rules. During the time she represents you as your criminal attorney, your attorney may be prohibited from accepting any interest in literary or media rights relating to the matter in which she is representing you.

However, if you offered the same attorney an interest in the literary and media rights to your book a year after the trial was over, in exchange for legal services in buying a house for yourself, she may be ethically permitted to accept payment on that basis, since the deal was made after the conclusion of the criminal matter.

MY FRIEND WAS A WITNESS IN MY CAR ACCIDENT LAWSUIT BUT SHE SAYS SHE CANNOT AFFORD TO TAKE A DAY OFF FROM HER JOB TO COME TO COURT TO TESTIFY. CAN I OR MY ATTORNEY REIMBURSE HER FOR HER LOSS OF TIME IN ATTENDING MY TRIAL AND TESTIFYING?

You or your attorney are ethically permitted to pay a witness for loss of time and reasonable expenses in attending a court hearing or testifying. If your friend was earning $100 a day at her job and she had to take two days off from work to testify, and she also incurred carfare of $25 for cabs to and from the court, you or your attorney would be permitted to pay her $250 for taking the time off to appear at your trial. If your friend was earning $400 a day as a physician, and she had to cancel all her patients for the two days she testified, you or your attorney would be justified in paying her $800 for making her two-day court appearance. You don't have to pay her; however, it is permissable to do so.

I NEED AN EXPERT WITNESS FOR MY AUTO ACCIDENT COURT CASE. SINCE I HAVE NO MONEY TO PAY THE WITNESS, I ASKED MY ATTORNEY IF THE WITNESS WOULD ACCEPT A FEE CONTINGENT UPON THE OUTCOME OF THE CASE SO THAT SHE WOULD ONLY BE PAID IF I WON MY CASE. WHY DID MY ATTORNEY TELL ME THIS IS IMPROPER?

Your attorney may be bound by ethical rules that prohibit him from knowingly allowing a witness to receive compensation based upon whether you win or lose the case, or based upon the content of the expert witness's testimony. This is to prevent a witness from slanting her testimony because of the possible money to be made if you win the case.

Imagine that you stood to gain $1 million if you won your lawsuit, and you promised the witness one percent of the recovery in exchange for her testimony. She might be influenced by the prospect of getting $10,000 for a few hours' work and lean favorably toward the outcome you want instead of being an objective witness.

SINCE I DID NOT HAVE THE MONEY TO PAY MY EXPERT WITNESS UP FRONT, MY ATTORNEY AGREED TO ADVANCE THE MONEY TO PAY THE WITNESS. IS THIS ETHICAL?

So long as you agree to be ultimately responsible for paying the witness's fee. Your attorney can also ethically advance court costs, investigation expenses, and other costs of your lawsuit if you agree to ultimate responsibility. So, if you had no money up front to pay your litigation expenses, but your attorney felt your case was a good one and agreed to advance your expenses, your attorney could put the money up for you to pay these expenses.

If your attorney advances fees for you, he'll have you sign an agreement to reimburse him. He can sue for the money if you fail to reimburse as promised.

CONCLUSION

TEN KEY POINTS ABOUT YOU, THE LAW, AND YOUR LAWYER

1. YOU CAN, AND MUST, TAKE RESPONSIBILITY FOR YOUR OWN LEGAL "HEALTH" AND WELL BEING.

This doesn't mean you have to become your own lawyer. It does mean that you have to make informed choices about the lawyers you choose, the legal strategies you follow, and recognizing your legal rights.

2. STAND UP FOR YOUR RIGHT TO ASK QUESTIONS.

You have to be persistent. A lawyer may not want or be prepared to answer all your questions. However, the legal system is based upon questions—you may have to remind your lawyer that he is not the only one who can ask them.

3. THE ONLY WAY TO GET THE INFORMATION YOU NEED IS BY ASKING QUESTIONS.

Don't be afraid to admit you don't know. Great inventions and scientific discoveries were made by people who "didn't know." They admitted to the world they didn't know all the answers; then they asked questions, questions, and more questions, until they found the answers they needed.

4. DISCOVER YOUR OPTIONS.

Options give you control over any situation. Never do anything, (or refrain from doing anything) just because your lawyer said so. Find out what your choices are, then make your decision.

5. KNOWLEDGE REDUCES FEAR AND ANXIETY.

It's not what we know that scares us, it's what we don't know. Legal difficulties can be very stressful, for yourself and for your family. You don't want to waste your strength and energy on imaginary or unnecessary concerns.

6. NEVER ASSUME.

Don't assume that you have all the information you need. A lawyer may have given similar instructions to 2,000 other people—but forget to give you one vital piece of information. Don't assume something is right for you just because a lawyer says it's so. Think about what you're doing, and make the lawyer think as well!

7. DON'T ACCEPT AN EASY ANSWER. PROBE AND CLARIFY.

Little children do this automatically. Answer a question and they'll come back with a "Why?" every time. You should do the same. You want to be sure you understand everything that's going on and that you are getting your money's worth for any legal services rendered.

8. A LAWYER IS JUST A HUMAN BEING.

No matter how intimidating she may seem, a lawyer really is just a human being. That means she can make human mistakes. She can also be warm, sympathetic, and understanding. Let her know what you need and how she can help you.

9. BUILD A ONE-ON-ONE RELATIONSHIP WITH YOUR LAWYER.

You don't have to become best friends, but asking questions sets up an immediate rapport with the lawyer. The lawyer's attitudes, as well as his answers, will give you important clues about his background and personality—and help you make a choice that is right for you.

Your questioning attitude lets him know that you're special and that you intend to establish a partnership with him concerning your legal affairs.

10. ASK SMART QUESTIONS. ASK SMART QUESTIONS. ASK MORE SMART QUESTIONS.

If you want to know more about Dorothy Leeds' speeches, seminars, and audiocassette programs, please call or write to:

Dorothy Leeds, President
Organizational Technologies Inc.
800 West End Avenue, Suite 10A
New York, NY 10025
(212) 864-2424
1-(800) 423-1169

Her Positive Action Cassette Learning Programs are the following:

Smart Questions: The Key to Sales Success. This unique and proven program will help you improve your questions to solve the mystery of the decision-making process, uncover the right information in the right way at the right time, practice surefire ways to answer objections, and close the sale.

PowerSpeak: The Complete Guide to Persuasive Public Speaking and Presenting. You can easily become a powerful and persuasive presenter by following Dorothy Leeds' proven PowerSpeak method.

The Motivational Manager: How to Get Top Performance from Your Staff. Being an excellent manager is the best way to get ahead. With this motivational program you will discover your strengths and weaknesses, how to hire, coach, train, motivate, and lots more.

People Reading: Strategies for Engineering Better Relationships in Business. Gain a huge career advantage by influencing others and achieving results through reading the unique differences in people.

INDEX